D1448374

Life Leverage

How to get more done in less time, outsource everything and create your ideal mobile lifestyle

Rob Moore

JOHN
MURRAY
LEARNING

This book is for everyone who wants to be somebody. For those who want to make a difference, for those who have the courage to stand up for what they believe in, for manically busy entrepreneurs, often misunderstood and willing to take risks because there's more to life than withering away slowly. This book is for you.

About Rob Moore

Rob Moore is a six-times best-selling author, having had three books reach number one out of all books in the world ranked on Amazon. Rob is perhaps best known for co-founding Progressive Property, the UK's largest property education company. In 2005 he was almost £50,000 in consumer debt, and within one year he co-owned a portfolio of properties that made him financially free, all bought with none of his own money. Rob became a self-made millionaire in his early thirties and now owns or co-owns over 500 properties.

Before the pivotal year of 2005, Rob tried his hand at a few enterprises and failed to make anything of them. He got a BA in Architecture that he did nothing with, became a pub landlord and struggled before he set up as an artist, which compounded his university debt and got him to within one month of bankruptcy!

Thanks to property, it took less than a year for Rob to first experience leverage. Rob leveraged his joint-venture partner's money for deposits, the bank's money to complete the purchases, the estate agent to find the property, the tenant to pay the mortgage and some cash flow, and the letting agent to manage the property. Rob had been used to working so much harder for much less money that it seemed surreal. Then the property crash of 2007 happened, and it all changed.

While most people struggled to survive, thanks to low interest rates, contrarianism and information leverage, Rob built Progressive Property, wrote his first Amazon bestseller, *Property Investing Secrets*, and was able to merge his passion and profession of property and business into one vocation and vacation.

Rob will tell you that he hasn't worked a day in his life since 2006, though in reality he worked harder than most at the start. But it wasn't until he really learned how to live the Life Leverage philosophy that he was able to create a fully autonomous, mobile lifestyle. Now in his mid-thirties, Rob is one of the UK's wealthiest and most successful 'disruptive entrepreneurs'. His property portfolio is fully managed and takes up none of his time, freeing and financing him to get two public-speaking world records and spend four months of the year in Grand Cayman, Florida, Monaco and Dubai. He doesn't even have an office in his office.

Rob now spends his time training trainers globally to grow towards his vision of global financial freedom, spending time with his fiancée and two young children, learning and writing. At three years old, his son Bobby was the youngest person ever to get a hole in one, and at four has recently qualified for three under-seven golf world championships. The greatest gift that the Life Leverage philosophy gives is time, with the people you love. Thank you for sharing this Life Leverage journey. If Rob can do it, you can too.

Contents

Section 3: Tactics

Section 4: Blueprint

Afterword: What are you going to do now?

Foreword: If it wasn't for you...

If you're anything like me, you probably just want to dive into the nuts and bolts, and you don't want to read long Oscar-speech-style thank-yous.

So let's keep it simple – thanks to Suneep, my amazing researcher, agent and friend, for his contributions to *Life Leverage*. Thanks to Heidi for her editing skills – blame her if there are any mistakes ;-). Thanks to Mark Homer, my supportive and analytical business partner; Gemma, the love of my life, for giving me freedom and love; my team at my companies who inspire me every day; and the Progressive community for your votes and suggestions in researching *Life Leverage*.

And thank you. Yes, *you*. You're committed, focused, inspired and you want to be better. You are willing to learn and grow and I'm very grateful to you for that, and for allowing me to be part of your amazing journey.

Let's get straight in.

Rob Moore, Disruptive Entrepreneur
www.facebook.com/robmooreprogressive

Introduction

Bob, not his real name for security reasons, was his company's best software developer. He was a family man and long-time employee in his forties, inoffensive and quiet. Someone you wouldn't look at twice in an elevator. He got glowing performance reviews and earned more than £120,000 a year. However, if you were to look at his web browsing history, you would find that Bob spent his working day checking sites such as Reddit, eBay, Facebook and LinkedIn and watching cat videos. He would write an email at the end of the day to update management about his 'work' and then would leave at 5 p.m.

His firm hired an investigator to look into some irregular work patterns and online behaviours, and they discovered that he outsourced his entire job and all the work he was hired to do to outsourcers in China. He did no actual work, at work. It wasn't clear how long Bob's scheme had been running because the log records dated back only six months.

Bob was paying a Chinese outsourcing firm about £25,000 a year to do his work. He would net £100,000 a year but had no work to do himself. In fact, it was believed he was also accepting freelance work on the side, contracting for other firms and then outsourcing that contracted work back to the Chinese outsourcer.

It turns out that his job and all of his work that he outsourced to China was above par – the employee's code was clean, well-written and submitted in a timely fashion.

He got fired for it!

If I had had an employee do this at one of my companies five years ago, I'd have fired them too. Not now. Now I'd promote them. Learn from them. Get their contacts from them, have a quick word with them about hiding it from me, and then have them head up a division where other departments and roles could be outsourced too.

Bob's story shows how times are changing, and the transitional conflict between previous conventional employment and corporate ideals is diminishing and a radical, new leveraged method of working, running an enterprise and living, is emerging fast.

Just 20 years ago, if you'd have seen me studying for my GCSEs, you'd have seen me working hard. My dad told me that, if I got all As, he'd give me £200 – a lot of cash to a 15-year-old and about £78,400 with inflation in today's money! Suckered in and bribed, I went for it, and revised morning and night. I sacrificed one full summer holiday, summer nights out with my mates and our friend Jim Beam®, and, of course, chatting up all the girls a teenage boy could wish for (or, rather, dream of). Because I really wanted that £200.

While I was buried under my books at the kitchen table, one of my best friends, let's call him Mark Homer for the sake of protecting his identity, was out every evening and weekend, having fun at the top of Cherry Hill, like all self-respecting teenagers should be. Mark was great with the girls, too, so I had plenty of reasons to be jealous.

'Just focus on that £200, Rob,' I kept telling myself.

Mark was in all my classes at GCSE level, and seemed to be quite relaxed about the exams. It was obvious he'd done no revision, yet seemed confident of passing with ease and grace. I'd sacrificed one of the best years of my life for my future, worked really hard, and resented him. At least he'd fail and my sacrificial decision would be vindicated.

When the results came in, Mark and I got together and tore off the perforated edges of our results. I read down my list of A, A, A, A, A, A … and felt amazing. I'd done it: £200 and a proud dad were my rewards. Now it was Mark's turn. He tore off the edges, peeled open the paper and read out his results: A, A, A, B, A, B …

Oh, no!

'How did you manage to do that, Mark? You didn't do any revision!'

'No, but *you* did!'

Turns out, he'd copied most of my exams. He didn't even try to hide or deny it. In fact, he seemed proud of it.

'You got great results and £200. I got great results, five girlfriends and the best year of my life,' he proudly told me.

Now, had he been found out, he'd have likely been suspended or expelled. He'd have definitely had his exam results revoked. That's the 'schooling' way. That's the way of the system most people are forced through. Just like Bob, he'd have been branded, ridiculed and made an example of.

I only learned the real lesson of this tale 12 years later.

In the real, modern world of business, Bob and Mark showed enterprise leverage. In the world of nature, that's called survival. In the world of attaining your vision, that's called outsourcing, getting a mentor, borrowing ideas and next generation/version/iteration.

I'm nearly over this event. It taught me a lot about the difference between the system and schooling and the 'real world'.

But it gets more ridiculous. Because of the grades I was expected to get at GCSE level, I was considered one of the more intelligent pupils, and was put in a new, special, top-set class. This class was called 'Géographie'. In this class, you were deemed smart enough to study Geography, in French. That's right: the entire Geography lesson, taught in French.

How useful this has turned out to be in the real world of getting ahead, running businesses and making a difference! Oh, yes. So many times, while serving customers, managing challenge and change and organizing my life and vision, have I called upon the deep resources learned at school in 'Géographie'. Well, at least I'd know how to turn left at the library and take the third right to get to the museum if I were ever stuck in Paris on my own.

So, if you want to go through the system that forces you to study hard for 18 years, get yourself £50,000 to £100,000 in debt in the process, get a low-paying apprentice-type job at the bottom of the career ladder and work your way slowly and painfully up for 40 years, then this book isn't for you.

If you want to work really hard, sacrifice all the time in the present with your family and loved ones, to put in extra shifts, to save some money so you can finally do what you want when you retire, rear-loading all your happiness and freedom, then this book isn't for you.

If you want to feel constantly overwhelmed, out of control, living a life making money and time for other people, continually stressed that there's too much to do and too little time, then this book isn't for you.

WHAT IS LIFE LEVERAGE ABOUT?

Life Leverage is about outsourcing all the things in your life that don't make you feel alive.

Life Leverage is about living your life to your highest purpose and vision.

Life Leverage is about living your values, your most important life priorities, to make money and make a lasting difference ...

... and reducing or eliminating anything and everything that doesn't serve that or isn't of the highest priority.

Life Leverage is maximizing the time you have on this planet to create the most vast and lasting legacy, eradicating wastage and tasks you can't do or hate to do, which still need to be done to achieve that legacy.

Life Leverage is living the things you are a master at, and outsourcing the things you are a disaster at. Growing in the areas of highest value to you, and letting go of everything else.

Life Leverage is a way of life, a modus operandi and a philosophy (explained later). It gives you constant clarity of purpose and vision, spontaneously present in your mind, and an inner knowledge of your most important actions and non-actions, priorities and posteriorities (explained later), in any given, madly busy, moment in time.

Live Leverage is happiness and fulfilment now, in the present, not delayed into a pension, retirement, or a later-when-it's-done-but-never-comes illusion. It's living your vision, purpose and legacy, now in the moment, while always growing to a higher level.

Life Leverage doesn't allow other people's urgencies and problems to become yours. It constantly questions convention and the 'way things are done', breaking the rulebook of 'hard work' and sacrifice.

Live Leverage is a genuine, non-delusional shortcut to high levels of success and achievement, with a disdain for duplication and 'lost time'.

THE 'PARTY LINE' OF SUCCESS

The party line of success is 'hard work' and sacrifice. Sacrifice the things you love, work harder and longer than anyone else, get up earlier, stay later, go harder, and you will be a success in the end.

Well, sure, that may be the case in sports that rely on physical strength or very specific skill/ability. That may be the case for very technical careers such as doctors and lawyers, but the 'work harder and longer' party line is a myth if you want entrepreneurial success, time freedom and Life Leverage.

There is a smarter way that the system does *not* want you to know about. Bob got fired for it. The system, the public sector and the standardized corporation will fine and punish you for it. They will brand you lazy and a cheat. They will make you feel guilt and shame for not working your ass off and giving your pound of flesh in time, hard slog and tax.

Do not fall for their power.

Do not fall for the delusion and brainwashing of hard work and quiet ignorance.

There is a better way – the Life Leverage way.

DARWINIAN TIMES

In business and technology, we are in a Darwinian 'survival of the fittest' seismic shift. We are moving fast through an Information Age into what is becoming a Technology Age. The Industrial Age, explained later, is well behind us. Anyone still relying on manufacturing or manual labour for their freedom and retirement is vulnerable, overworked and underpaid. They got left behind years ago.

This Technological Age is fast. *So* fast. In the blink of an eye, global interconnectivity and remote productivity have taken over for the early adopters and entrepreneurs who embrace it. You can start any business, anywhere in the world, from a small device you hold in your palm. You can tap into free Wi-Fi, set up a shop or business with no need for staff, inventory or stock, virtually no overheads, and on someone else's server or cloud. You can access a billion customers or followers for free, across the globe, as quickly as you can communicate. You can leverage social and marketing platforms and media fast – and for free. You can grow multi-million- and billion-pound enterprises aggregating other people's ownership, stock and responsibility. Alibaba.com, the world's largest e-commerce platform, holds no stock. AirBnB owns no hotels. Uber owns no cars. Facebook creates no content. Netflix owns no cinemas.

Social platforms that have made zero actual sales have floated for billions. Twitter's initial IPO (Initial Public Offering) sold $14.2 billion of stock and there was no revenue model. Facebook raised $104 billion in its 2012 IPO before they added Facebook ads to their platform. These companies set up by teenagers in student digs are selling 'ethereal promises' and 'future sales' for billions. Coders and hackers are the new celebrity rich. Anyone can post a video and get millions of views if they have a strong enough opinion. Our social lives are now in the public domain. We can get anything we want at the touch of a button. Tech has even become intuitive and knows what else we want; it can literally read our minds and recommend things we didn't even know we wanted. It knows how to make us addicted.

The gulf between the old and the new is widening further and further. Embrace the new technology age, or become extinct. The Life Leverage philosophy merges easy-to-use technology with a lifestyle of freedom and autonomy. The Life Leverage philosophy shows you how to get maximum benefit from this new Technology Age with minimum personal effort and time wastage, how to leverage it for your personal and business life, how to get more done in less time, outsource everything and create your ideal mobile lifestyle.

WHAT YOU CAN EXPECT FROM THIS BOOK

Life Leverage is not just another 'time management' book. It is a life philosophy of getting more achieved in less time. Maximum leverage: minimum wastage.

Life Leverage is not just another 'outsourcing' book that gives you a few websites and ways to hire on the cheap but only works until the next new craze comes along. It is a way of sustainably leveraging, outsourcing and hiring out every single thing in your life that doesn't add maximum value and benefit to your vision and legacy. It is a way to have 'freedom' and 'retirement' now, not later. You get to have perpetual 'mini-retirements', rather than hoping you will get one big long one in 20, 30 or 40 years; that rarely comes for most people.

Life Leverage is psychology, a way of thinking and feeling in the moment to maximize success and progress, with fulfilment – not the emptiness or dissatisfaction of always striving for the elusive more.

The Life Leverage philosophy gives you clarity to be spontaneously tuned into your purpose, to build a legacy and make the difference you know inside you are meant to make. It is your heads-up dashboard display, like having your own cockpit, helping you to keep growing and progressing while living your highest values in each moment. You will intuitively know to do only that which is of highest importance, because you are more 'balanced', in control and in flow.

You can expect a new, modern way of thinking differently, innovatively, and always seeking the shortest route to the best result. Become redundant, not reliant. Master time. Question convention. Rebuff the pressure people around you put on you to bail them out and do things that are urgent for them but not for you.

You can expect to control and balance business/work, family and children, passions and making a difference/giving back equally and effectively, on your terms, without sacrifice or decades of delayed gratification.

You can do what you love and love what you do, merge your passion with your profession and your vocation with your vacation.

Life Leverage has four main sections:

1. Concept
2. Strategy
3. Tactics
4. Blueprint.

Concept covers the Life Leverage philosophy, architecture, attitude and way of thinking about life (leverage). It introduces the anti-system mindset and methodology.

Strategy describes the grand design, direction, vision and approach towards your life of leverage by design – on purpose.

Tactics covers the operational, nuts-and-bolts techniques to 'get more done in less time, outsource and live a mobile lifestyle' – the details and specifics that serve the concept and strategy.

Blueprint describes the 'Mobile Lifestyle' master plan model: the Mobile Lifestyle Blueprint (MLB), the systems, apps, software and architecture to design and operate a remote – anywhere in the world – mobile, passive income, free time, lifestyle.

AND THANK YOU ...

Thank you for having the faith in me to help you on your journey to your ideal mobile life. I congratulate you for investing in yourself wisely. YOU are your best asset and you pay yourself the best interest and return.

As a thank-you I have two special gifts for you, very valuable and lever-age-able, hidden within this book. I am certain you will be one of the smaller percentage who will read the book from start to finish; after all, those who don't read have no advantage over those who can't read.

Abbreviations used in this book

IGT: Income-Generating Task

IGV: Income-Generating Value

KPI: Key Performance Indicator

KRA: Key Result Area

MBL: Mobile Lifestyle Blueprint

OPM: Other People's Money

OPT: Other People's Time

VA: Virtual Assistant

VVKIK: Vision, Values, Key Result Area, Income-Generating Task, Key Performance Indicator

Section 1: Concept

This section, which is about the concept of Life Leverage, covers philosophy, architecture, attitude and a way of thinking about life. This is the anti-system mindset and methodology of Life Leverage. Like the great architects who have a single concept for a building, or the best-selling books that have one single, recurrent theme, or the niche businesses that serve one sole purpose and don't try to be everything to everybody, and the band that creates a great riff or chorus that they repeat throughout the song to make it catchy, your entire life by design is built on the Life Leverage concept.

Life Leverage: how to get more done in less time, outsource everything and create your ideal mobile lifestyle.

#1 There's no such thing as 'time management'

'Time management' as a concept is utterly ridiculous. It must surely be one of the most misunderstood concepts in work and life. The more you think about 'managing' time, the more of a slave to it you become. It's like trying *not* to think about something you are thinking about only making you think about it more.

You cannot manage time. It does not stand still for anyone. It does not wait. You cannot control it in anyway. Time will keep going, it doesn't care about you, and it will take you with it in the end.

So how come there are so many time-management books and gurus? Perhaps it's because everyone is looking for the shortcut or time hack to beat, and save, time. It was Brian Tracy, perhaps one of the world leaders in the tactical field of time management, whom I hold in very high regard, who first taught me what 'time management' is:

TIME MANAGEMENT IS LIFE MANAGEMENT

You don't 'manage' time, you 'manage' yourself. You manage your life. You manage your decisions, behaviours and emotions. This book isn't called 'Time Leverage', it is called *Life Leverage*. It's about leveraging elements of yourself and your life, to make it appear as if you have more time.

We all get graced with enough time on this planet to do amazing things that can leave a legacy for generations to come. If one person can reach the Moon, make a billion, get a PC into every home, rid the world of polio, become the world's best bodybuilder then highest-paid actor then state governor, in their lifetime, then so can you. Bill Gates and Arnie have the same number of minutes in an hour, hours in a day, days in a week, weeks in a year, years in a decade as you.

So it's never about how much time you or anyone else has or hasn't, and all about how you choose, use and invest that time, that makes all the difference – the difference between being somebody and being anybody.

If you miss a deadline, it wasn't that you didn't have enough time; you didn't manage your workload or workflow well enough. You weren't disciplined enough to do what needed to be done in the time that you had, which was enough when you started.

If you don't do something that's important to you, or you can't balance all the things in your life, then you aren't managing your priorities effectively. If you feel you are running around doing things for the benefit of other people and not for yourself, making other people rich and not making yourself happy at home, or you are confused, frustrated and overwhelmed, then you this is down to you. You allowed time to do that and blocked time to do the things that make the biggest difference to your life (your vision).

If you get to the end of the day and think to yourself, 'Did I actually get anything meaningful done?' and the answer is 'No', then you wasted the greatest gift and the most scarce and valuable resource known to humankind: time.

Time is our most valuable and precious commodity, slowly running out, slowly catching up on us. Time is being invested or wasted. There is no 'in between'. Time is your currency, asset and mechanism of value and exchange. You can only 'manage' time by managing your life and how you invest the time that you have, which is equal to the time everyone has. Time is currency and how you can cash in on that currency has its own chapter, coming soon.

Life management is discipline in action. Discipline isn't about pain, self-negation or sacrifice as much as it is about having a vision: a longer-term view of who and where you want to be, and making the right, highly prioritized decisions moment to moment, even when you don't feel like it in that moment.

Life management, previously known as time management, is about leveraging other time-related assets such as people, capital, ideas, information, software, systems (all explained in detail in Life Leverage strategies in Section 2) to maximize your results and benefit to you, 'burning' away as little of your own time as possible, so you can invest the maximum amount of your own personal time as possible, according to your highest values and towards your vision and legacy.

CHEATING TIME

You 'cheat' time, or get more done in less (of your personal) time, through outsourcing and leverage. Not through working harder and longer. You 'cheat' time through understanding time as asset and currency, not as tasks, to-do lists and what you have to get done.

You 'cheat' time by being clinical about highest 'priorities' and lowest 'posteriorities' (low or anti-priorities); single-mindedly focusing on highest-value or highest Income-Generating Tasks (IGTs), and delegating, delaying and/or deleting everything else.

Summary

You can't manage time, you can only manage your life. In the rest of this book, the 'how to' tactics of preserving and leveraging time for maximum productivity will be revealed. So will the intuitive, spontaneous understanding of your highest values, your life's vision and the legacy you want to leave behind that guides your efficient investment of time, never wasting a second or getting pulled into other people's urgencies.

view of what and where you want to be, and making the right, blurry-prioritized decisions moment to moment, even when you don't feel like it in that moment.

Life management, previously known as time management, is about leveraging other time-related assets such as people, capital, ideas, information, software systems (all explained in detail in the Leverage strategies in Section 2) to maximize your results and benefit to you, 'burning away' as little of your own time as possible, so you can invest the maximum amount of your own personal time as possible, according to your highest values and toward your vision and legacy.

CREATING TIME

You 'cheat' time, or get more done in less, for your personal time, through outsourcing and leverage. Not through working harder and longer. You 'cheat' time through understanding time as asset and currency, not as tasks, to-do lists, and what you have to get done.

You 'cheat' time by being clinical about highest 'profique', and lowest posteriorities (low or anti-priorities), single-mindedly focusing on highest-value income Generating Tasks (IGTs), and delegating, delaying and/or deleting everything else.

Summary

To 'cheat' personal time, you can only leverage wider use, by being clear of the nagging, the value of time as an asset by creating more you don't have to 'read' nearly will be rewards, so will the future. economic rational creation of real global values, will the way to do, rewarded when leveraged and focus, and invest as you value and it is a 'creation' time, never wasting or stealing or truly replacing time of other people's time.

#2 Time currency

Time is the real, universal currency. Before money was exchanged in a 'fiat' system, and even before the introduction of coins and precious metals, before governments controlled the monetary system, people would exchange their time to create a product (a cobbler or smith, for example) or provide a service that someone else perceived to have value. If they didn't, they likely died, unless they could hunt, because they'd have no mechanism to buy food.

Individuals would exchange their own product or service that they had exchanged their own time and passion to create, and these would be exchanged in turn for other products or services. When there was no universal monetary system to regulate fair exchange, you had the manifestation of your time invested as your one and only currency.

The value of that currency was directly related to the value of the time invested. And the value to the recipient of that time invested was their perception of that value, *not* yours. So time, as a currency, is in fact how recipients of your manifested time investment perceive the value of it to them and/or their life. They will then exchange something they value in return for it. This is known as 'fair exchange'. Fair exchange is the natural and agreed right balance between buyer and seller, giver and recipient, during a sale and purchase where a transaction happens.

Currency literally means 'flow'. Currency is an always-moving value exchange of time investment. Money is the end result, but currency is the continual flow of time between interconnected people. Just as money flows from one person to another to another very quickly, so can, and does, your time. You make more money by creating more currency, also known as economy, enterprise or GDP (gross domestic product), all of which are the flow of time in monetary form.

If fair exchange doesn't take place, or the balance is at either extreme of the spectrum in favour of the buyer or seller, one party feels that they're not valued highly enough, or that they are being cheated. In this instance, time as currency loses its value and circulation, where the buyer who feels cheated looks for compensation and tells others of their experience, or the seller who feels undervalued can't sustain funding their free time or can't make profit with high enough prices to pay their overheads.

THE IRONY OF TIME

The irony of time is that most people can't or don't measure time, and therefore place a real value to it. You can't master what you don't measure. Instead, they place value on material items or financial mechanisms, spending or wasting all their time to get a very physical remuneration.

Society raises and forces you down a route convincing you the right way to live is to work hard your whole working life, exchanging all your time for a small amount of money to just get by and just pay your bills, taking overtime and sacrificing free time, so that you can save up or buy free time later in life, to do what you always wanted to do. But when you get to your later years, you start running out of time, and the money you thought you'd saved for retirement is less and doesn't last. So you have to work longer and harder, never getting those years back. Then, when you finally can retire to do the things you love to do, you die.

Society in the industrial age set up three stages of 'life' related to work: learning, earning and yearning years. Learning years are 0–18, earning years are 18–65-plus (it used to be 50) and yearning years are 65 to the end of life. You're sausage-machined into going to school and learning to get a job or career, and encouraged to work most of your life to set up some free time right at the end, *if* you get there.

There's an illness or phenomenon known as 'Broken Heart Syndrome'. Its more official name is Takotsubo cardiomyopathy. This is a syndrome or illness where the heart temporarily enlarges and doesn't pump well, causing shortness of breath, angina and sometimes death. It is a physical reaction to a surge in stress hormones that can be caused by an emotionally stressful event. This 'Broken Heart Syndrome' is one of the main killers of people when they 'retire'. They literally die from sudden loss of purpose, belief and hope, caused by no vision and their lack of financial provision.

This must *not* be you. This would be such a sad and empty way to die. You should die having lived a long and exuberant life that made a huge difference to others, and go out in a blaze of glory.

WARNING: the learning, earning and yearning societal system is an outdated model. This is the antithesis of Life Leverage. This is the way most people in the world understand and are forced down, but it is *not* the only way.

THE ALTERNATIVE – THE LIFE LEVERAGE WAY

The Life Leverage way means that you can earn in the learning years. You can teach your children about business and money from four years old. You can put audios on in the car, get them watching educational YouTube videos on the tablet at a young age, and they can start setting up online businesses and earning money at 13 years old.

The Life Leverage way means you can keep learning in the earning stage of life. Don't stop learning just because you've finished school. Continually investing in your education and knowledge will ensure that you continually get a return on your time and increase your financial reward.

The Life Leverage way means that you don't have to wait to your yearning years to 'retire'. You can do what you love and love what you do, make your passion your profession and your vocation your vacation.

Work doesn't have to be work, and you can take 'mini-retirements' every week or every month, you can 'front-load' rather than 'rear-load', or delay, your retirement. You don't have to have all work at the front of your life (front-loaded) and all retirement at the end of your life (rear-loaded). I 'retired' twice, in 2007 and 2009; never again, it was so boring! It was like eating Italian with no carbs. I lasted no more than a month before I needed a purpose. I didn't want to start my slow decay. I know now that I just had the wrong definition of 'retirement'. I had defined retirement the way society defines it, and not how it really should be for someone who controls his or her own life and time.

You can now 'work' remotely and mobile, anywhere in the world, while on vacation. You can mix business with pleasure, and social with operational. You can merge passion and profession. You can redefine both. Work doesn't have to be work any more.

Life Leverage means that you don't have to wither and die in your yearning years. You don't have to reminisce or wish you'd seen your children grow up or you'd done more with your life, or not worked as hard.

Here are the five biggest regrets of the dying:

1. I wish I hadn't worked so hard.

2. I wish I'd had the courage to live a life true to myself, not the life others expected of me.

3. I wish I'd had the courage to express my feelings.

4. I wish I'd stayed in touch with my friends.

5. I wish I'd let myself be happier.

With the Life Leverage philosophy, you don't have anything to 'retire' from. You don't have the shock of total boredom and lack of purpose.

Your vocation and vacation are already merged, so you keep living your life with equal balance between work and play, and you live longer and more happily. You're not reliant on a financial or governmental system that has wasted your retirement fund.

Life Leverage merges your learning and earning years and removes your yearning years completely, other than for the fact that you'd yearn for another equally fulfilling life to live all over again.

You can write the rules of your life. You don't have to delay everything you want to do until your time runs out.

As you will learn later, there are various leverage models to maximize time while minimizing wastage. There are laws of time that, if you obey and leverage them, will give you the maximum benefit. You can do, be and have more in less 'spent' time through the Life Leverage philosophy.

Summary

The Life Leverage philosophy is about allocating time to things that give you the greatest return, enjoyment and freedom, which maximizes time leverage and minimizes time wastage. Time is the single most valuable currency and a commodity that can be eroded or leveraged. See time like other currencies, investing and protecting your time, exchanging it for only the highest-priority functions that are the most important to you.

#3 The 3Ms of your emotions

If time management isn't time management but rather life management, then life management is emotional management. How you manage your emotions 'manages' the results in your life.

If you have control of your emotions and you take responsibility for them – accepting a balance of emotions, controlling negative emotions and making strategic rather than reactive decisions, then you will live a life you love; a life by design.

The 3Ms of your emotions are:

Stage 1. Misuse

Stage 2. Manage

Stage 3. Master.

STAGE 1: MISUSE

Misuse of emotions is being an effect of them, rather than a cause of them. It is being controlled by them, rather than controlling them. Have you ever done anything that you later regretted? Have you ever reacted badly to a situation and treated someone in a way your calm, controlled self wouldn't have? Of course you have, because we all have. For many people this is a pattern that plays on repeat throughout their life:

Step 1. You feel strong emotion.

Step 2. You react negatively to someone based on that emotion.

Step 3. You regret it later.

Step 4. You start again.

Most people are slaves to their emotional reactions, and this is the single biggest factor that spirals their life out of control. It is the one main block to success and the single biggest contributor to unhappiness, low self-esteem and broken relationships.

In fact, sadly, most people don't even know that they can control their own emotions. To them it is who they are – an auto-conditioned response to a situation that just happens and over which they have no conscious control. This is not a 'personal development' or emotional management book, so let's keep emotional management relevant to Life Leverage:

- Do important tasks first.

- Be single-minded on one, most important, task at a time without task-jumping.

- Do the hard things first and fast.

- Manage your own time and don't be pulled around by others.

- Be honest with yourself that you're doing the highest-value task.

- Compartmentalize your time so that vision and strategy time get done first and are not put off for operational or firefighting tasks.

- Know your energy highs and lows during the day and put the right priorities or posteriorities in each time compartment.

- Isolate yourself from all distractions and create force-field time.

The above are examples of practices that will take you from Stage 2, managing your emotions, to Stage 3, mastering them (looked at in detail below).

STAGE 2: MANAGE

You manage your emotions when you become aware of them. You have your good days and bad days. Everyone does. But you are able to have conversations with yourself, give yourself feedback, and you know 'intellectually' the right and wrong way to spend, invest or waste your time.

You're smart. This probably isn't the first 'how to' book you've read, and you probably know a few time-saving, time-management tactics. The thing is. you're still too busy, not getting enough done, your to-do list is growing, you're feeling overwhelmed, trying to balance out all the work–life–health–travel–family commitments and not being as great at any of them as you'd like to be and know you could be.

> *'To know and not to do, is not to know.'*
> – Anon. (Someone smart. Someone Zen.)

You may be juggling too many tasks or sidelining money-making ventures, getting stuck with admin tasks, or feeling like you can't let go. It is time to hire or train others to do the things you don't like or aren't great at.

STAGE 3. MASTER

When you master your emotions, you know how you will feel before you feel it. You know what pushes your buttons and you don't put yourself in that position (or you make sure you're in a padded cell and strait jacket when you are). You know when you are on fire and in a fire, in or out of flow, and you know how to plan and predict how the outside world is going to try to disrupt the master plan you wrote last month, last week and last night.

You know what you're a master at and what you're a disaster at (and you're OK with your weaknesses). You have a clear vision of how you want your life to be, you know your hierarchy of values and you know the legacy you want to leave and be remembered for. You constantly plan and check in on your vision, values, KRAs (Key Result Areas), IGTs (Income-Generating Tasks) and KPIs (Key Performance Indicators), making important time for strategy and vision and delegating or dumping low-value tasks. You stay poised and calm in a crisis, looking for solutions to problems and how you can serve others, rather than demanding power or importance.

MASTER-TASKER

When you are the master of your emotions, you manage yourself and your business more effectively. Below are eight examples of practices that masters use when approaching task-setting and becoming a master-tasker.

1. Doing important tasks first

Even if in that moment that task is long or hard, you know that this gives you the highest value, so you just crack on and get it done. Perhaps you break the task down into manageable chunks, or give yourself mini-targets and mini-breaks.

2. Being single-minded on the one, most important, task at a time without task-jumping

Each time you feel like checking emails or Facebook, you say no. You talk to yourself, managing yourself, and you stay focused on the one task at hand. You know that overwhelm is thinking about all the bumf you have got to do, and the ONLY way to get rid of it is to focus purely and solely on the task at hand, because that is the quickest route to getting through your big to-do list.

You know that each time you 'task-jump' there's huge wastage in starting the task again and getting your brain back into momentum and flow. Staying single-minded on the task saves time and gives you momentum.

3. Doing the hard things first and fast

You don't put off hard or painful tasks; you do them now. You attack them head on and you smash through them. Or, as Brian Tracy says: 'Eat that frog.' If the worst thing you had to do to start your day was to eat a live frog, the rest of the day would go much better. How anyone came up with that random analogy I don't know, but it's become synonymous with getting the hard, big, nasty tasks done first *before* you've had time to talk yourself out of it or it's grown in size, festered, stressed you out and got even harder.

You know that once you have eaten that 'frog' you will feel a great sense of satisfaction or relief. That will send endorphins, 'happy hormones', off to your brain and give you a great feeling of achievement and self-esteem that will create momentum to move up to bigger things.

You know that discipline is doing what you know you have to do, even when you don't feel like doing it. While doing it you, imagine how you'll feel afterwards, and it gives you the boost you need to get on with it.

4. Managing your own time and not being pulled around by others

You know that the world will pull you from pillar to post with your pants around your ankles, unless you plan your time according to your vision, values and KRAs. You know how to politely say 'No', to not get dragged into anything that isn't a high priority, and you know that, if you don't have a plan, you will become part of someone else's plan. You know not to believe most people when they tell you how urgently they need you, and you have ways of isolating and gate-keeping your-self from persistent time drains.

5. Self-honesty that you're doing the highest-value task

You know that you're the easiest person in the world to lie to. You know you can convince yourself of anything, and justify anything with a lame excuse or story. You know that by saying 'tomorrow' you actually mean 'never'. So, you don't believe your cheeky inner voice that tries to convince you that you've 'worked hard' just because you've pushed paper around for eight or nine hours. You're able to prioritize efficiently and ruthlessly without blaming, complaining or justifying.

6. Compartmentalizing your time so that vision and strategy tasks get done first and are not put off for operational or firefighting tasks

You know that vision and strategy time are the most important 'tasks' you can do. You know that communicating that vision to others in your team and training them is also a high-priority task, and you know that, when you're busy, vision and strategy time can get dropped because it doesn't seem as important or urgent as operational tasks that need doing *now*.

So you compartmentalize your diary, putting in evergreen time each day or week for high-level strategy, vision and planning time, and you *never* miss it or let anyone else delete or block it out for operational or firefighting tasks. Details on what to compartmentalize and how to do it will be explained later.

7. Knowing your energy highs and lows during the day and putting the right priorities or posteriorities in each time compartment

You know how to game and trick yourself. You know you will be bang on it after a coffee and when you first wake up, so you diarize vision, strategy and high-KRA/IGT time at those times. You know you will have a carb-coma at 1 p.m. to 3 p.m. so you put low-value or admin tasks in then, won't kill you if they don't get done. You prioritize the highest value tasks and times in your highs, and posterioritize the adminy, itty-bitty tasks in the lows.

8. Isolating yourself from all distractions and creating force-field time

You know that if you need to focus on high-KRA and -IGT tasks, it's best to turn off email, turn off the Internet and social media if these aren't part of the task, and, most importantly, position yourself spatially where no one can interrupt you. Don't tempt yourself. If you want to succeed in dieting, you're best off emptying the fridge and cupboards, and the same goes for getting important things done.

I didn't log into Facebook or check any emails during the writing of this section.

Because you're the easiest person to lie to, why rely on yourself to 'manage' yourself? Why not get a coach, mentor or mastermind? Why not have someone who is invested in your success, knows your vision and will hold you accountable to a higher level of success and achievement? Every single successful person I've ever met or studied has had a coach or mentor, or both, or many. More on how to achieve this later.

Summary

The 3Ms of emotions are: Misuse, Manage and Master. Mastery of emotions is not about becoming a machine, never feeling pain, negative feelings or weakness. It is about knowing yourself, second-guessing how you will feel and when, and setting up your lifestyle, environment and systems to assist your focus. Manage your emotions, manage your life – master your legacy.

#4 The hard-work delusion

One of the biggest mythical delusions that you hear from the standard 'how to be successful' mantras is that 'you have to work hard'. Work harder and longer than anyone else, and you will be the best. Make sacrifices and go the distance. Never give up. Keep going when it hurts. Don't be weak. Man up. Smash it.

While this may be the case in conditioning for strength or sports at the very highest level, there are way more things to consider when choosing your vocation and investing your time.

Firstly, you have to choose the right path to invest time in. It's pretty insane to work hard and long and make huge sacrifices in a vocation that is unlikely to yield results. And that is what most of the planet is doing – in a state of being walking dead, shoehorned by society.

If you put in 60 hours a week in the hope that you will get a promotion every three to five years and an incremental pay rise that doesn't even match inflation, and you delay the gratification of doing the things you love with whom you love when you love and where you love, and it is clear that it takes 30 years to get your salary from £30K to £60K, then working harder and longer is delusional.

If you give half your waking life to a technical skill that could become redundant with technological or cyclical changes, and you rely on state systems to look after you in your 'yearning' years, then working harder and longer is delusional.

If you spend your time working to make someone else rich, without the direct ability to control the financial upside, then working longer and harder is delusional.

The almost universal delusional assumption is that time and money are directly related. That is, that the harder and longer you work, the more money you make. This is not the case, because of diminishing time and the diminishing law of return.

THE OVERTIME MYTH

And then, to make a little more money, the employee (you?) works overtime. Overtime is another delusional concept, that you are making more money when in reality you are exchanging more of your time with diminishing returns and benefits. It's time you can't ever get back, for a sum that you just spend on more material items and increased personal overheads, putting you in a no better personal financial position, but instead incrementally increasing your overheads. This brings more pressure as more money has to be earned just to stay in the same previous financial position, but it now takes more (over)time to achieve, while inflation creeps up behind you.

Conventional thinking gives conventional results. The conventional employee with the conventional mindset of 'work hard and take overtime' does create wealth and enterprise, but most of that is for the owner of the business, or for the state in taxes. Employees are elegantly trapped by mortgages and overheads and the delusions of security and a 'safe' retirement, but the fact is that at any time, without warning, the state could spend your pension, one single regulation change could make your job redundant or one decision from your boss could put you out of work.

AN UNHAPPY AND UNHEALTHY WORKFORCE

From research, here are the most common feelings/dislikes of employees:

- I don't feel appreciated.
- I have no clear purpose for the company.

- I don't feel I make any difference.

- My boss doesn't care about me.

- I feel like I'm a number.

- My job expectations are unrealistic.

- I don't have enough breaks to recharge or focus.

And, according to the University College London (published in *The Lancet*): those working a 55-hour week face a 33-per-cent increased risk of stroke than those working a 35- to 40-hour week. The longer the working week, the higher the risk of a stroke. Those working between 41 and 48 hours had a 10-per-cent higher risk of stroke and those working 49 to 54 hours had a 27-per-cent increased risk. They also have a 13-per-cent increased risk of coronary heart disease.

All this so that they can 'retire' when they are 65?! They may not even get there.

PENSIONS

The 'pension' statistics get worse:

- 99.7 per cent of over-65s in the UK do not have pension plans.

- 88.2 per cent reaching retirement age will rely on the state pension system, which does not have enough money to pay them.

- £824 a month is needed to be saved today if a typical 30-year-old wants to retire at 65. With the average UK salary at £25k, that's almost half their monthly wage.

- A 30-year-old today retiring at 65 and relying on the state pension would get only £7,500 per year / £145 per week.

- A £30k pension pot gives only £35.81 per week.

- The average shortfall of pension savings facing UK citizens is 37 per cent.

- 29 per cent of the UK population has no savings, 46 per cent of savings are held in low-interest bank accounts and 65 per cent of adults are not saving for retirement.

- Pension fund deficits among FTSE 100 companies are so large that one-third will never meet them.

- Within FTSE 100 companies, £2 of every £3 is spent on past deficits rather than current employee benefits.

- A £100,000 pension pot will buy an annuity income of just £5,750.

There's not a lot of proof out there that most of the employed population are happy, healthy, wealthy, fulfilled and valued. They feel that they have no freedom or choice, they can't control their destiny and have a deluded sense of 'security' that is, in fact, the biggest exposure to risk they could probably have.

TAXES

When you're an entrepreneur, you take all the money upfront. You charge your client, add VAT and take the cash in. You get to keep the VAT for the government for a few months before you owe it to them. You can even earn a bit of interest on it. You can claim the VAT back on any business purchases you make. Then you run as many viable costs through your business as you can that you are allowed. There are many more offsetable business expenses than most people know. In fact, many of them are in black and white on the HMRC website.

The corporation tax you will owe is paid up to 18 months in arrears, after you have offset as many costs as you can and drilled your profit down. You only have to pay personal tax when you draw the money, and if you structure your company as a limited company, you can take dividends and lower your salary. If you structure a limited-liability partnership, you only pay personal tax on drawings, much of which can be offset too.

However, it is a very different story for employees. The personal tax, National Insurance contributions and student loan repayments are taken at source before you ever get paid. The only way you ever knew you really earned it was that it was printed on your payslip. You think you earn a six-figure salary but you pay almost half of it in tax. You never even see nearly half that money. You have no offsetable expenses and no chance to get that tax down.

So you get 55 per cent of your salary in the bank. Then you pay 20 per cent of the cost of fuel in tax, 20 per cent of the cost of food, alcohol and tobacco in tax, 20 per cent of the cost of clothes, electricals and meals out in tax, 2–12 per cent of (most of) the purchase price of your property in tax and council tax to live in it.

Then you're basically forced to insure many of these items, such as your car, your house, and its contents, cat, dog … chicken? There's a tax premium of 5 to 17 per cent on insurance. In effect, you are being taxed twice – the insurance and the tax on the insurance – a premium on the premium.

Then, if you actually make any money, you pay capital gains tax on any 'capital gains'. These taxes are currently between 18 and 28 per cent minus a few minor exemptions.

And, to cap it all off, when you die, up to 40 per cent of your estate above a few hundred thousand (which would buy a garage in Kensington or Chelsea) is taxed.

If you take all the taxes off a £60,000-a-year salary, you are taxed between 60 and 70 per cent of your total income as an employee. This is not good news. You're getting paid last, after the government, after your bills and subscriptions and overheads: stone-cold last. You get to have around 35 pence in the £1 to live on.

EMBRACE THE NEW AGE OF BUSINESS

It's actually not as tough as most people think now to control your own financial and emotional life. The Internet gives us all the world's information organized in a way that is easy to find and consume. At the touch of a key you can hack into a free Wi-Fi connection, you can set up online e-commerce accounts such as Amazon or eBay for free, you can sell some old possessions you don't need any more and raise some small start-up capital, to buy and sell some more. You don't need any premises or stock or overheads. You can raise more finance online from peer-to-peer and crowdfunding sites.

You can find all your customers online at a low cost or free through social media sites. You can build a brand, a reputation and a raving fan base for your business or passion that can go viral and global, online, for free, from anywhere in the world. You can set up apps or technology fast and at low cost. You can run your entire business from one device. You can receive money fast with the flash of a card or a phone at the speed of light through fibre optics.

And yet most people think it's hard. The only three explanations I can see for the mass delusion of hard work is that:

- most people don't know how to create Life Leverage

- they don't think they can, or

- they don't think they have a choice.

In this book will show you that:

- you can learn how
- you (or anyone) can
- you *do* have a choice.

MAKE THE CHOICE NOW

Imagine if there were no risks to starting again. Imagine if you were guaranteed all the help you needed along the way to do what you love and love what you do. Imagine if you could create your ideal work–life balance. Well, you can – now.

Here's how:

1. Choose a vocation with a path of least resistance and limitless upside that *you* control.

2. Choose a vocation that's also a vacation and a profession that's also a passion.

3. Study what the most successful people whom you admire or idolize do, and copy (most of) it.

4. Know what to keep going at, and what to give up on.

5. Make the Life Leverage philosophy *your* philosophy

Let's look at each of these in detail:

1. Choose a vocation with a path of least resistance and limitless upside that *you* control.

This is the real definition of security. If your current career or vocation is limiting you, then you're in the wrong place. In the 'if you could start again with no risk' scenario, you'd probably choose a vocation where the earning potential was limitless, the roles/positions/career path was limitless, the number of customers was limitless, your ability to make a difference was limitless, your (global) reach was limitless, freedom and creativity and enterprise were limitless, and your ability to grow was limitless.

What's stopping you from making this choice today?

You probably wouldn't choose a vocation where over half your income was taxed, taken at source before you even see it. You probably wouldn't choose a career that takes 35 years to become a junior partner and which could be instantly taken away from you by a 'senior' person or a change in regulations.

So what's stopping you from making this choice today?

2. Choose a vocation that's also a vacation and a profession that's also a passion.

You have nothing to run away from, take time off from or 'holiday' from if you do what you love and love what you do. Why does it have to be that you spend most of your waking life doing something you hate in order to buy a bit of time and earn a bit of money to do what you love with the remnants of what's left?

It doesn't have to be that way. You can choose to merge your passion and profession, or find the roles within your profession that you're best at and you love (most of the time), and outsource the rest the Life Leverage way.

Remember this scenario of starting again with no risk? Of course, you'd pick something to do that you love to do, without the fear that you couldn't make enough money from it. How you create 'passion–profession merge' is detailed later.

3. Study what the most successful people whom you admire or idolize do, and copy (most of) it.

Your idols are likely to have created a life you want, and therefore have learned, as perceived by you, to merge passion and profession, live a life according to the Life Leverage philosophy, get more done in less time and outsource all lower-value tasks. If they can do it, you can too. Most of them are self-made, and most of them idolized someone before you idolized them.

So, one of the easiest, safest and quickest ways to create your ideal life is to study them/theirs, leverage their journey to fast-track yours and model or copy what they've done to be where they are.

This concept is so simple you'd think everybody would do it. The problem is that people think it's too hard, that they can't do it, that the idols had it easy, or they are just envious and resentful of successful people. But the reality is that most of us start quite equal, and the successful find systems and strategies that get them to where they want to be within the shortest, most leveraged time frame.

Wealth is a relevant example, as money is something that most people are interested in and want more of, and that seems to have an extreme polarization of distribution. A recent Oxfam report says that half of global wealth is held by 1 per cent of the population. Data shows that the share of the world's wealth owned by the best-off 1 per cent has increased from 44 per cent in 2009 to 48 per cent in late 2014. The least-well-off 80 per cent currently own just 5.5 per cent of the world's wealth. And you know who moans about this the most? It certainly ain't the wealthy!

On current trends, the richest 1 per cent will own more than half the world's wealth in the next two years. The richest 85 people ('the global elite') on the planet between them control as much wealth as the poorest half of the global population put together. The 'global elite' share a combined wealth of £1 trillion, as much as the poorest 3.5 billion of the world's population.

The wealth of the richest 1 per cent amounts to $110 trillion (£60.88 trillion), or 65 times as much as the poorest half of the world. So which Life Leverage 'strategy' are you going to learn? The 1 per cent way or the 99 per cent way? If one person can become self-made, you can become self-made. So start now.

4. Know what to keep going at, and what to give up on.

In the next chapter of *Life Leverage,* there's a section on 'giving up'. In the general whoop-whoop rah-rah world of personal development and success, giving up is seen as a weakness. But giving up is *only* a weakness if you give up on something of high value, return or importance. Giving up is actually the smartest, strongest and most courageous thing to do if what you are doing is of low value or has a low return. Don't keep going at something for hours, weeks, months or years, as I did with my Architecture degree, just because 'giving up' is weak. You will learn to intuitively know what to push through and what to give up on.

5. Make the Life Leverage philosophy your philosophy

Know what to do, and do what you know. Don't get sucked in by someone else's plans for your life. Don't follow the walking dead crowd. Live life your way, on your terms, on purpose with the Life Leverage philosophy of getting more done in less time, outsourcing everything of low value, and creating your ideal mobile life.

Summary

Society, standard 'personal development' and 'self-help' would have it that working harder and longer than anyone else will make us better, richer and happier. This is a delusion. You just end up making sacrifices and burning yourself out for a retirement you can't afford and have no time left for. Your results and ideal life-style come from life leverage, working strategically and systematically, maximizing your time to focus on your vision and being ruthless around mindless work and time wastage.

#5 The myth of 'balance'

Another ridiculous concept that is assumed to be common sense by the masses is 'work–life balance'.

How can it be 'balance' that you spend more than *one-third* of your entire life – or even as much as 50 years – 'working' to rear-load (delay) all your happiness and free time to the end, which may not even happen, and certainly not for as long as your 'working' life or 'earning' years.

That's more time working than sleeping! That's more time working than the total sum of playing, exploring, creating, sharing, giving, being, learning and loving. That's not balance, that's self-imposed slavery. That's not what you would wish for your children, so why accept it for yourself?

How can it be 'balance' when you do many things to the extreme that you hate for such a long time, and you do so few things to the extreme that you love for such a short time?

How can it be 'balance' that you spend all week sacrificing yourself for a short weekend doing what you really want?

Weekdays working and weekends off are a societal imposition. Starting work at 8 a.m. and finishing at 6 p.m. is corporate imposition. Having to 'work' to 'earn' a living is a capitalist imposition. Doing the work one month in advance and getting paid one month in arrears and having all the tax and National Insurance taken off you upfront is a governmental imposition. Do you have to live life following rules imposed upon you by another person or a system?

No, you don't. You *do* have a choice, if you know another way. If you know the Life Leverage way.

THE SWING OF THE PENDULUM

A pendulum swings from one extreme, through the centre, to the other extreme. It actually spends very little time 'in the middle'. It takes most of its time to get back from one extreme and, once at the middle, it passes through it quickly and moves towards the other extreme.

This is how work–life 'balance' and focus really work. Where focus goes, energy flows and results show, but where there is no focus things start to rot. You can never balance time and tasks, hoping for the pendulum to stay in the middle – that's insane. Sometimes you will have the pendulum at the work extreme, where you are in control of your money and career, but not spending as much time as you'd like at home. At other times, you will have a great home and family life but your career is stagnating or you aren't making enough cash. This is how time, life and focus work; it doesn't come in equal measure and equal balance but in extremes of 'focus or forget', 'grow or decay', 'master or disaster'.

People who master their time and live a life they control break those rules; they create their own rules. They know another, better way. Did you ever see a hyper-successful person talk about work–life balance? No? They never 'moaned' about 'working' because they either loved to do it or didn't love to do it in the moment but had a bigger vision to guide them through it. It's not that successful people don't feel pain, or get to do everything they love all the time, it's that they have a clearer purpose, they are grateful to serve and solve, and they intuitively know what they are meant to do, even if it is painful in the short term. They know how to flow with the swing of the pendulum.

BREAKING THROUGH

Here are ways to break through always feeling that you haven't mastered the work–life 'balance':

1. Don't separate 'work' and 'life' (a weird concept anyway).

2. Have a clear vision of, and for, your life.

3. Give up on low priorities.

4. Let go and say 'No'.

1. Don't separate 'work' and 'life' (a weird concept anyway).

Work is life and life is work; it's all one and the same. Life doesn't stop when you're at work, and work doesn't stop when you're 'at life'. Sometimes when you're working, you get to do fun things you love that make you feel valued and purposeful; sometimes when you're doing what you love, you have to do things you don't enjoy that are painful and humiliating. You can't run away from either extreme of emotion, so it's delusional to think that all work is pain and all non-work is joy. Follow where the pendulum swings, focus moment to moment on the one focused task at hand, and do that as best you can. If it's something you love or a nasty task you have to get out of the way, do that thing as best you can.

To get most of the happiness, freedom and control most of the time, choose a profession that's also a passion – a vocation that's also a vacation. If you do this, you don't have to have 'work' at one extreme of the pendulum and 'life' at the other extreme. Merge work and life to become one whole, where possible and practical. Enjoy 'working' when you're at 'home', and take holidays and social trips when you're at 'work'. Take perennial 'mini-retirements' and don't rear-load them. 'Work' longer and harder because you love doing it and want to make a difference and make something of yourself. Don't leave family at 'home' and work at 'work': involve your family and your hobbies in 'work'. Be more mobile, so that work and home and travel aren't so compartmentalized where it's assumed you're 'stressed' at 'work' and 'chillaxed' on holiday.

Break the rigid, society-imposed structure and create your own that suits your life and your vision. If you become obsessed, as most passionate, successful people do, it doesn't have to have such a huge 'cost' in terms of a 'childhood' or 'family time' or 'friends'. Why have 'work friends' and 'home friends'? Why not merge them all together? Live it all now in the moment, so you don't have to delay or 'balance' any of it and you don't have anything to run away from. Don't live weekdays and weekends; live anything, any time, anywhere.

2. Have a clear vision of, and for, your life.

Find something to be obsessed about that you are meant to do, that can give you great self-esteem and purpose, and that will make a difference to other people. If it doesn't, don't do it. Don't be all things to all people. Drop stuff. Become extreme – extremely focused on your vision and purpose, and extremely unfocused on everything else.

Work isn't work when you're doing something you know you are meant to do that can make money and make a difference. Work isn't work when your passion is your profession. Work isn't work when you have a person to grow into and become, and a vision bigger than you to ensure that each day you get up equally challenged and satisfied. Tuning into your vision and values is coming soon in *Life Leverage*.

3. Give up on low priorities.

Giving up is seen as weakness. And giving up on the pursuit of a worthy goal, when you're often so close, results in an 'easy in the short-term, painful in the long-term' outcome.

Giving up early when it gets a bit sweaty is often a sign of weakness. It may show a lack of vision and long-term perspective. Starting again, again and again is a surefire way to get nowhere but take a huge amount of time doing it. But sometimes wanting to give up is feedback that what you're doing doesn't really matter to you. Why keep going doing something just because giving up is seen as weak, or because you're nearly there towards nowhere important?

I started a BA in Architecture and I knew in my heart after two weeks that it wasn't what I really wanted to do. I kept going for another 154 weeks because I didn't want people I'd never met to say to themselves when I wasn't there that I'd given up. They didn't even know me, so why did I even care? Go figure!

In my case, I was stupid *not* to give up. Those almost three years cost me almost six years of lost opportunity, which could have taken me somewhere more meaningful.

Give up, now, on things that aren't important. Just drop them. You won't die. Give up on the things you're not going to succeed at. Give up on the things you hate but feel pressure to keep doing. But never give up on things that make a difference to you just because it gets hard. Vision, self-awareness and wisdom come from understanding the difference. Are you one step away from a goal that's important to you or far down a road that isn't?

4. Let go and say 'No'.

Don't do or be things because other people expect you to be or do something. External peer pressure is tiring and incongruent. Let go of low-value, unimportant things that don't serve your vision and values. Leave it to someone else (who may love it and be great at it). Get out of their way. Leave them alone. Let them fly and don't micro-manage them.

You'll see how liberated you'll feel when you drop things, admit that you can't do everything, and put that time and energy and passion into something meaningful that will make a difference to you, those you love and those you serve. People are going to judge you whatever you say or do, so say and do what is right for you, maintaining grace and humility.

For more on this, see Chapter 16.

Summary

Trying to achieve a work–life balance is futile. Your life swings like a pendulum, rarely in the centre and most often moving towards the extremes. Where focus goes, energy flows and results show. The answer is to merge your passions and profession, your vocation and vacation. Don't make sacrifices and create your own rules, not the usual work hours or constraints made by employers, society or external expectations. Do the things you love according to your values and vision, drop time-draining distractions, say 'No' more and live the Life Leverage way.

#6 Leverage defined

Leverage is an art form in a scientific guise. Put simply, it is about achieving more with less. More money with less money. More time with less (of your personal) time. More results with less (of your personal) effort. It's also known as the 'law of least effort' and/or the '80/20 Principle'.

> *'Give me a lever long enough and I could move the world.'*
> – Archimedes

To many, this concept is just not believable. They've been brainwashed to believe that 'working harder' means that you'll earn more money. You have to 'graft' and 'sacrifice' in order to 'earn a living'. However, living is your right: you don't have to 'earn' it; you should be living it.

Everyone experiences leverage. You either leverage or you are leveraged. You are predator or prey. You are employer or employee, slave or master, leader or follower. Each serves the other, but one leverages and the other is reverse-leveraged.

You see, you're either utilizing leverage in your favour, moving towards your inspired vision, earning on OPM (Other People's Money – bank, joint-venture partner), getting results on your time invested and OPT (Other People's Time), or this is happening to you, in reverse, and you're working for someone else's vision, being leveraged by them, getting paid an hourly wage for time you've given up (and will never get any residual benefit from).

If you work for someone else and you're not happy, or you work for money and that money stops when the work stops, and no one works for you, then you are being controlled by others' leverage. They are earning from you; you're bottom of the food chain, earning the least and working the hardest. You probably have the least control and freedom, and you're possibly the unhappiest. Most people are brainwashed into thinking that time, work and money are directly related, but millionaires, billionaires and business owners know that they are inversely related. You're taught to work hard for money, but you need to make your money work hard for you. You're taught that longer hours and overtime earn more money, but in reality vision, leverage, leadership and team building earn the most.

THE PROOF

To prove that time and money are inversely related, here's some data on the highest- and lowest-paying jobs, according to the Office of National Statistics tables of national salaries:

The highest average salary for a career in the UK is a broker, earning on average £133,677. Brokers don't even create their own products; they sell others' and earn a share of the sale. Brokers therefore have lower overheads and lower risk, and they can change the product they sell whenever they decide. They can work from home and can focus on selling the products with the highest commission and lowest amount of effort. If it all goes wrong, the company they were brokering for is likely to take the hit.

A broker on average earns 24 per cent more than the next most highly paid jobs, which are chief executives and senior officials, earning an average of £107,703. These roles are very strategic, often involving leadership, team building, meetings, travel, vision, and more thinking effort than physical or manual labour.

At the opposite end of the earning league table, at numbers 349, 350 and 351, are care escorts, playworkers and school-crossing patrollers. These roles have a high level of responsibility, involving sensitive care of children or vulnerable people. Between them, they earn a yearly salary of £5,853, with school-crossing patrollers the lowest at £3,394. These roles are very hands-on, exchanging time for money with zero leverage, often outside in the winter, working over Christmas and fully responsible for other people's health and safety. The average earnings of these three roles are 22.84 times lower than the highest-paying role.

It's not only the amount of money that is extremely polarized; it is the number of worked hours and the ability to delegate.

According to the *Wall Street Journal*:

- 44 per cent of the wealthy worked 11 hours fewer each week than the poor

- 86 per cent of the wealthy who had full-time companies worked 20 hours a week, whereas 57 per cent of the poor worked 50 hours a week

- 65 per cent of the wealthy delegated work, managing three to five sources of income.

Now this is not to say that working for someone else is wrong. You can earn well and still work less in an employed position, as shown by brokers. We all need one other, and we are all interdependent. The banks need the borrowers and the borrowers need the lenders. The landlord and tenant need and serve each other. The cleaner needs the boss and the boss needs the cleaner. And if you're happy at the 'hand-to-mouth' end of leverage, then you're happy, and you're not going to be judged by me. You're probably just reading this book for fun and you'll go back to living a happy working life.

But perhaps that is not you, and perhaps you want more, but you don't want to kill yourself doing it, or make huge sacrifices over the things you love and the people you love. Perhaps you have a greater vision. Perhaps you want to leave your mark and legacy on this planet when you're gone, inspiring and financially fuelling many generations to come.

DEVELOPING LEVERAGE

Of the 25 richest people in the UK, none of them is an employee. All of them are founders or recipients of businesses. They are all employers, business owners and investors. Every single one.

If you can master and control leverage, then you will be wealthy beyond all your expectations, plans and goals (and quite possibly your dreams). You will earn money and preserve time by using other people's time, resources, knowledge and contacts.

This is what millionaires and billionaires know and do. It's the biggest worldwide myth that you have to work hard for money; you need to make your money work hard for you. Just look at the billionaire lifestyle and tell us whether they are working 'harder' than the slaves, the cleaners and the servants. Here's the good news: what they know regarding leverage is learnable. You can learn the same strategies and systems that they know and have learned, and are using to make money, preserve time and make a difference.

Leverage is becoming more and more important in our society. First there was the wheel, the donkey, the camel, the horse and the elephant. Did prehistoric man use the mammoth to get from his ice house to the local ice bar? You get the picture; humanity leveraged animals to make a journey quicker and easier.

Then there was the wheel, 3,000-odd years BCE. Then came the bicycle, then the train, then the car, then the plane, then the shuttle. Fibre optics send information and money at the speed of light so we can leverage the Internet and the world's information, organized by Google!

Who knows what will come next, but whatever it is will make journeys even faster and easier, thanks to compounding and Moore's Law (not Rob Moore!). You can outsource any task for pounds and pence on sites like elance.com, peopleperhour.com, fiverr.com, onlinejobs.ph. You can employ a VA (virtual assistant) whom you can pay by the hour or even by the minute, to do tasks for you to free your time to focus more on Income-Generating Tasks (IGTs). If you spend five hours a week leveraging non-IGTs that might cost you £40, those five hours can be spent building your business or buying a property that might bring you in £30,000, and thousands per year in passive income for the rest of your life.

Let's use the example of investing in property, seeing as it is one of my passions and business ventures. You have the 'entrepreneur/investor' type and the 'landlord' type. While investors do have landlord duties (regulation, management, maintenance), landlords are hands-on, unleveraged 'workers'. They are simply self-employed people whose job it is to buy, manage and maintain properties, and they aren't that much better off than they would be in a well-paid job. They often get involved in refurbishments, painting and decorating, collecting rent and other operational tasks. Of course, these tasks are important, necessary and, were they not done, the properties would not produce cash flow. The entrepreneur/investor, on the other hand, keeps to the high-level strategy and vision and leverages, outsources, employs, begs and borrows (at the start) all these regulations, management tasks and maintenance to/from others, freeing their time for higher-level IGTs, and staying focused on their vision and living according to their values.

This example/analogy is the same in most other niches or industries. You can use the Life Leverage philosophy for maximum leverage and time preservation, or you can be the hard worker at the bottom of the food chain, burning your life away and feeling like a slave to your business.

Leverage really is easier and more accessible to the everyday person than it used to be, mostly thanks to the leverage of the Internet. The main things holding people back are lack of knowledge, lack of belief, overwhelm, information overload and fear. It can be a hard shift for many people who are ingrained with values passed on from their hard-working parents from a different era/age of 'get a job, work hard, get your head down, make sacrifices and don't take risks'. Then many self-employed people (who think they are business owners, but are really slaves/ employees to themselves, their employees and their customers) take real power, ownership and control of things that they have built. They have identity and importance from being the boss and getting stuck in; they can get precious about handing tasks over to other people because no one can do their job as well as they can; they think they can't afford to pay people to do things, or that they can 'save money' by doing it themselves.

Of course, I'm not saying that's you, but perhaps you can relate to this?

A DIFFERENT STRATEGY

When we first get into a niche, industry or vocation, we tend to think that hard work and graft, and doing everything ourselves to minimize costs, is the best way forward. While it does stop wastage of costs, it creates wastage and de-leverage of time. It also involves doing a lot of things you didn't sign up to/for, when the reality kicks in. But you don't know what you don't know, so you listen to society drumming into your brain 'Work hard ... Work hard ... Work hard' over and over again.

When I first got into property, I thought that viewing properties, going through the purchasing process, dealing with mortgage brokers, refurbishing, renting out and managing tenants were going to be my daily vocation (grind). After a dozen purchases and well on the way to financial security in my first year, I suddenly woke up and asked myself 'Is this really what I want to do with my life?' The reality was that I wanted the baby but *not* the labour pains. I personally did not enjoy the nuts and bolts of property, but I was knee-deep in it now, and I was making money.

Without a vision and leverage, property can be a job like any other, if you let it, with unpleasant stuff to deal with and people who don't value you. But it also puts people regularly on the rich list once they know how to master leverage of time, money, resources, ideas and people.

I decided then that I didn't want to run my property business like a part-time overworked landlord, and looked at ways I could get other people to view, offer, buy, rent, refurbish, manage and maintain my properties, while still making a fair share of the income. And it's not that I was trying to pass the buck, because, as I found out from working with Mark Homer, my business partner of ten years, there are people who value these tasks, even love them, and earn their own living doing them. Talk about a revelation! So, if I could leverage this all out, that would mean I could grow, earn more, do more of what I love, *and* create commerce, jobs and economy. And other people would love doing what I hate. A real win–win solution. There is more later on how you can achieve this too.

Leverage is the non-get-rich-quick, get-rich-quick(er) strategy for business and life. It is the real, non-get-rich-quick shortcut to success, freedom and time preservation. Your success and scale are down to how much or how little you leverage, and this section will help you start with your outcome and vision clear in your mind, and give you the shortest possible route to Life Leverage, how to get more done in less time, outsource everything and create your ideal mobile lifestyle.

You see, when I first started my first real business in property (I don't count being an artist because I didn't have a clue about business then), my business partner and I did everything ourselves. We probably didn't do too badly because we kept costs really tight, we protected the downside and we reduced risks; after all, just as we'd set up shop, the biggest recession/property crash in history happened. But, looking back, we could have achieved more, faster and smarter, without increasing risk too much, if we got out of our own way and leveraged out most of the boring and difficult jobs to others (far better at them than we were), at a much lower rate of pay than for us doing it ourselves. This would then have freed us to do more IGTs and compound our income, results and legacy.

This is shown in how fast many of the students and community members of Progressive Property, my property training company, get results – the proactive ones do so well so quickly if they pick up on leverage early, and fast. Many of them are now full-time property investors. Many of them build (multi-)million-pound property portfolios in six, 12 or 18 months. Many of them hit net passive income figures of £3,000, £5,000, £10,000 or £20,000 in one to three years. Many quit their old jobs. Many of them are even now training others and are respected experts in the industry, giving back and making an additional income stream. Many of them achieved results quicker, faster, better and with fewer mistakes that we did when we started, because they leveraged our time investment in property.

If you'd have been with us in December 2006, you'd have seen us sourcing our properties, arranging and doing the viewings, finding the tenants (to save the money on fees – poor leverage), checking the properties, even doing the maintenance, painting and decorating and ongoing management. We were also doing all our websites ourselves, our own admin, management accounts, post, going to networking events; you name it, we did it, ourselves, the hard way. And we both did the same thing, so there was zero-per-cent leverage and 100-per-cent duplication! 'Sweat beats regret' – we said.

After a year or so, the time we were spending doing everything was actually holding our business back, costing it money, and repelling huge amounts of money we didn't know we were losing, because we couldn't see it. We didn't know the opportunity cost of what we weren't doing, because we couldn't see it. We didn't know what we didn't know.

The results you get and the money you earn aren't as much about what you are doing, but what you are *not* doing. If you're not doing what the wealthy are doing, you aren't going to get the wealth they get. But we thought we knew better. We bought into the old, conventional wisdom of working harder, working longer and making sacrifices. We were in so deep we had no view outside. No one was steering the ship but it was going at full steam heading nowhere in particular.

The business couldn't grow because we only had so many hours in the day. No matter how many hours we worked or how hard or even how efficiently we worked, we kept hitting the ceiling. As we got so busy, our time was taken away from IGTs, and we started making mistakes through fatigue and lack of focus. We were doing the wrong things well and often, and the right things not at all because we were too busy to do them. We kept getting in our own way.

And besides, the whole point of working for ourselves was so that we could free up some time to do the things we really loved, right? But we were too busy working to be able to do these things, and the dream of financial independence and time freedom was starting to slip, despite buying around 20 properties in our first year in partnership together. We were very busy, full-time, de-leveraged landlords – slaves to a small business.

We thought that this was how every business was! Work hard or go home. We didn't realize that it was our behaviour. We didn't understand leverage because we were going it alone. We didn't have coaches, mentors or a network of experienced businesspeople. We just got our heads down.

With hindsight, we needed to create our business so it would work independently of ourselves, if it were to grow, and be congruent with our lifestyle and vision. We wanted passive income, a scalable portfolio and to help others achieve the same. We couldn't do that on overdrive hard work. We needed to continually increase our IGV (Income-Generating Value) by ensuring that we were totally strict about what we did, outsourcing all low-income-level tasks, and only doing what had the absolute highest IGT to us. Anything that brings in less than our personal IGT (you'll work out yours later) must be outsourced, or you go backwards and become poorer, but working harder for that right.

Fast-forward to now, and business for me, and for our companies, is a leveraged business. In fact, Progressive has become eight separate businesses to include lettings, personal development, speaker and e-commerce training, money lending, commercial buying and more. Our portfolio has grown from 20 properties in year one to almost 600 in Year 8. Each year compounds. Group turnover has gone from zero to tens of millions of pounds. Staff has gone up from our mums to between 50 and 100. We now run nearly 600 training events a year, and not just in the UK; many of these take place in buildings we own personally and lease to the company. This is not said to impress you; many of my mentors and friends are at a larger scale, which in turn inspires me. But there's no way on earth I could have done the above 'on my own' or with 'hard work' alone.

When we started we did everything, and it cost us a lot of money. I'd say we'd be twice the size if we started again, read this section, and stuck to the rules and models I'm sharing with you following the Life Leverage philosophy.

This is just as important in your private life, too. If you iron your clothes, that's time taken away from making money. If you cut the grass or clean the house, that's time away from IGTs. If you drive to an event rather than have a driver or get the train, that's dead time you can't leverage or earn from.

I once read a book that said that millionaires cut their own lawn. It was an old book, and I feel that this is a bit of out of date now. If a millionaire can do a property deal in a few hours, time spent on non-IGTs actually blocks out and repels the IGTs. You save £30 mowing the lawn but leave £30k on the table by not doing a deal. And that's what the mass population do, because they can't see the opportunity cost of what they are *not* doing and where they are *not* spending their time.

Perhaps the millionaire cuts his or her own grass to create a strategic vision in peace, away from the humdrum world. Now that's leverage and NeTime (No Extra Time – explained in Chapter 18). Perhaps they had an audio on while they were doing it, for double leverage?

I now have a full-time chef (my mum) – she cooks and I pay her credit card off each month. She's a trained chef; we get to see each other every day. And if you saw me iron a shirt, you'd see me lose seven months off my lifespan, 17 minutes wasted and burn marks in perfectly acceptable stripy Duchamp shirts. Yet pop down to Peter's Cleaners and you get three shirts pressed for £5. That's cleaned and ironed! And send the housekeeper to get them and hang them up. That's 51 minutes saved, seven months of your life back and £5 invested. In 51 minutes we could probably make five or six figures doing some kind of property or business deal from that £5 invested (as long the time was reinvested wisely). Plus, we add to the financial and resource flow of the economy in our area and support local businesses, too, giving many hundreds of people jobs, houses and contracts, which we believe will, in turn, come back to us through the laws of economy. This is known as 'fair exchange' and more is created doing higher-level IGTs than lower-level ones.

You may think that it's OK for me and all those rich business owners – we're in the position to do that, and you don't have the resources that we do. You have overheads and children and mortgages and responsibilities and no time. Yes, exactly. The longer you leave leverage out of your life, the longer people leverage you and the longer you stay poor. Live the Life Leverage philosophy or be leveraged.

In later chapters of *Life Leverage*, you'll get the specific, technical 'how to' details about Life Leverage. Make sure you get all the way to the end because some of the specific techniques are towards the end of the book.

Summary

Leverage is achieving more with less, using other people's time, money, experience and network. Leverage and outsource now, even before you are ready. Invest your time rather than spend it and use NeTime to fill wasted time with leverage. Get used to getting other people to do things for you, without guilt or concern for the cost. Think 'Who can I get to do it?' Build a team. Manage. Lead. Don't focus on low-value tasks because the compounded opportunity cost is huge. Embrace leverage and you can free or buy back time and utilize that saved time to make more money and do the things you love, now.

#7 The 80/20 Principle

In 1906 the Italian economist Vilfredo Pareto created a mathematical formula to describe the unequal distribution of wealth in his country, observing that around 20 per cent of the people owned 80 per cent of the wealth. In the late 1940s Dr Joseph M. Juran attributed the 80/20 Rule to Pareto, calling it Pareto's Principle.

More generally, the Pareto Principle is the observation that most things in life are not distributed evenly. The 80/20 Rule also became the guideline to relative distribution. It can be more extreme, such as 90/10, or sometimes, in the case of wealth distribution or relative success, 95/5, or 99/1, or in the case of millionaires versus non-millionaires 99.987/0.003.

The 80/20 Principle, in short, is the unbalanced, uneven distribution of benefit/drawback and success/failure, and is very much part of the Life Leverage philosophy.

Here are some areas where 80/20 is in play:

- 20 per cent of the input creates 80 per cent of the result.

- 20 per cent of the workers produce 80 per cent of the work.

- 20 per cent of the customers create 80 per cent of the revenue.

- 20 per cent of the bugs cause 80 per cent of the crashes.

- 20 per cent of the features cause 80 per cent of the usage.

- 80 per cent of value is achieved with 20 per cent of effort.

- 80 per cent of wealth is owned by 20 per cent of people.

- 80 per cent of your complaints come from 20 per cent of your customers.

- 80 per cent of sales come from 20 per cent of your products or clients.

Later, Richard Koch wrote a book called *The 80/20 Principle: The secret of creating more with less*. He states that 'The 80/20 Principle is one of the great secrets of highly effective people and organizations.' Taking Pareto's Principle into the modern age, studying how to create more with less in an overworked, unproductive era, Koch says:

- A minority of inputs leads to a majority of outputs.

- Focus on the few activities that produce the majority of life satisfaction.

- Most of what we do is low value – eliminate or reduce the 80 per cent of efforts that produce poor results.

- A minority of causes create a majority of effects.

- Identify and build upon the critical few – the 20 per cent of efforts that produce 80 per cent of the results.

- In business, focus on the products and customers that make you the most money, and minimize or eliminate the rest.

- A minority of decisions will produce the majority of your results: your choice of work, debts, investments and relationships.

- More effort does not equal more reward – focus only on what is crucial, and ignore the rest.

A UNIVERSAL LAW

I have found this principle to be uncannily, almost spookily, accurate. In studying wealth distribution, I believe Pareto uncovered a universal law across everything that you can be on the right side of for Life Leverage, or on the wrong side of for overwhelm, confusion, frustration and painfully slow results. It is two sides of the same coin, two halves of the same whole, in that it can work 80/20 or 20/80, and seems to manifest in all areas of our lives. For example:

- You use 20 per cent of your apps 80 per cent of the time.

- You wear 80 per cent of your clothes, 20 per cent of the time – maybe many of them still with the tags on.

- 80 per cent of your hair is in 20 per cent of the area; for men, 80 per cent of your baldness is in 20 per cent of the area.

- You get 80 per cent of your happiness from 20 per cent of the things you do (and vice versa, for most of the planet).

- 80 per cent of the wear of the carpet is in 20 per cent of the room.

- 80 per cent of the wear of a car engine is in 20 per cent of the whole engine.

- 80 per cent of the wear on your keyboard is on 20 per cent of the keys.

- 80 per cent of the return on your stock portfolio will be from 20 per cent of the investments.

If you agree that this principle is powerful and prevalent in all life areas, then, in order to get more done in less time, outsource everything and create your ideal mobile lifestyle. We have to condition ourselves to think, decide and act 80/20.

The 80/20 Rule isn't about working harder, it is about working selectively, smarter and with ruthless efficiency, so you can preserve time. The Life Leverage philosophy is inspired by 80/20, and observes the 80/20 Principle in all areas of life.

In summary:

- Don't waste 80 per cent of your money for 20 per cent gain.

- Don't waste 80 per cent of your time for 20 per cent enjoyment.

- Don't do 80 per cent of inefficient tasks for 20 per cent completion.

- Don't network with 80 per cent of the people you meet.

- Drop 80 per cent of the things on your to-do list.

- Do 20 per cent of the things that matter to you, 80 per cent of the time

- Delete, delegate or drop 80 per cent of your emails and demands on your time.

Later on, you will learn models and systems to efficiently and ruthlessly organize and prioritize your time for maximum leverage and time preservation, according to your highest vision, values and legacy. You will also learn how to 'manage' yourself in de-prioritizing (posteriorities), letting go and saying 'No'.

Summary

The Pareto Principle says that 80 per cent of your results are achieved using 20 per cent of your time and it seems to apply to everything you do. Since 80 per cent of the wealth is held by 20 per cent of the people, how can you invest your time wisely on your highest KRAs and IGTs to get 500 per cent (five times as much) of your results using just 20 per cent of your time? Be ruthless, avoid all time-draining, low-value tasks and focus on maximum leverage.

#8 The Life Leverage philosophy

The Life Leverage philosophy is a way of living your life to get more done in less time, outsourcing everything and creating your ideal mobile lifestyle. It is a way of thinking, feeling, deciding, doing, and then getting the results and feedback accordingly, to build momentum and get closer to your vision and legacy.

Life Leverage doesn't 'end' with sitting on a beach drinking piña coladas, or retirement, or freedom, or balance. It allows you to live that way from moment to moment – or whatever that 'end goal' is to you – now, and not rear-loaded, merging your passion with your profession and your vocation with your vacation.

It also means you don't get 'Broken Heart Syndrome' or a lack of fulfilment when you do 'get to the end', because there is no end to rear-load, and by the time you get there you've done everything you would have wanted to do and you don't want to run away from the career; so you just keep living the Life Leverage philosophy.

The Life Leverage philosophy is about living a fulfilled and inspired life, with passion and profession in balance, and without overly sacrificing either. The Life Leverage philosophy doesn't understand 'work–life' balance or separation; it merges every aspect into one inspired life.

The Life Leverage philosophy understands and accepts the balance of ups and downs, happiness and sadness, and moves towards its vision and legacy, constantly tweaking and accepting feedback. It disdains duplication and waste, getting maximum leverage and maximum time preservation with minimum time erosion and wastage. It doesn't rear-load retirement; instead, it lives continual mini-retirements.

The Life Leverage philosophy is in tune with your vision (V), values (V), Key Result Areas (KRAs), Income-Generating Tasks (IGTs) and Key Performance Indicators (KPIs). This is your VVKIK, and you should be constantly checking in right from V up to K, and intuitively aware of the right thing to do.

The Life Leverage philosophy questions the conventional way things are done, is sceptical of 'normal', and is continually and with a contrarian eye looking for the shortest yet most sustainable way to your vision.

The Life Leverage philosophy does not let other people's emergencies become yours. Instead of thinking 'How can I do it?' or 'I can't do it', you ask 'Whom can I get to do it?' You ask for suggestions before questions, you become redundant not reliant, and outsource everything in your life that doesn't make you feel alive.

Life Leverage is about living your life to your highest purpose and vision. It is about living your values: your most important life priorities to make money and make a lasting difference ... and reducing or eliminating anything and everything that doesn't serve that or isn't of the highest priority.

Life Leverage is maximizing the time you have on this planet to create the most vast and lasting legacy, eradicating wastage and tasks you can't do or hate to do, which still need to be done to achieve that legacy.

Life Leverage is living the things you are a master at, and outsourcing the things you are a disaster at. Growing in the areas of highest value to you, and letting go of everything else.

Live Leverage is happiness and fulfilment now, in the present, not delayed into a pension, retirement, or a later-when-it's-done-but-never-comes illusion. It's living your vision, purpose and legacy now in the moment, while always growing to a higher level. Life Leverage helps you get more done in less time, outsource everything you need to outsource and create your ideal mobile lifestyle.

Summary

Living your life according to the Life Leverage philosophy means you can live a fulfilled and inspired life, enjoying every day, doing the things you want to do, while making a difference and serving others, now. Not when you're 60 or even 50, but right now. You can merge your passion and profession, your vocation and vacation. You can have it all as long as you have a vision, live your values, serve others and live the Life Leverage philosophy.

#9 The Law of Compounding

Money attracts money.

It is said that like attracts like, and money is no different. Albert Einstein called the Law of Compounding the eighth wonder of the world. He believed it was a law – a universal principle that can be observed, well, universally.

Imagine a little bet on a golf course: betting £1 per hole and doubling your bet on each hole seems like a fairly innocuous challenge. However, that £1 bet compounded over each hole turns into £256 in nine holes.

That's quite a compounded effect, isn't it? Well, that's nothing. After hole 15, that amount has compounded to £16,384. Look at how much more money is being attracted now, in a shorter time, because of the compounded effect. Once you get to hole 18, the compounded total is £131,072.

Assets work the same way. Cash flow works the same way. Business and enterprise work the same way. Branding and reputation work the same way. Knowledge and education work the same way. And, most importantly, hidden in the background pulling all these strings, time works the same way.

A species of water lily also obeys this rule, it seems. Each day it covers double the water surface it covered the day before. The first few days it covers very little that is visually or tangibly obvious. But after 30 days it has covered an entire pond or lake, regardless of its area. This means that, 29 days in, it had covered only half the size of the pond or lake. It took 29/30ths of the time to get 'halfway' and 1/30th of the time to get 'all the way'. It took 28/30ths to get a quarter of the way there, 27/30ths to get an eighth of the way there, and so on. This idea is revelatory and can be leveraged to gain huge momentum, if understood, honoured and implemented.

The Law of Compounding states and dictates that the maximum benefit and momentum come the longer you are in or doing it, rear-loaded nearer or at the end.

THINKING LONG-TERM

In order to gain maximum Life Leverage from compounding, you need as long a time perspective as possible. People who think from hour to hour earn a wage and spend it. People who think from day to day are employed to carry out functions imposed upon them by managers who can think from week to week. Higher-level managers may plan month to month, performing the yearly plan of the highest-level managers. The highest-level managers are implementing a vision created three to five years into the future by the owners of enterprise. These enterprise owners are inspired by the visionaries who can think and see time in decades, and these visionaries are inspired by the sages who can see into next generations or lifetimes. The scale and reach of the vision is therefore directly related to the length of the time perspective.

On 25 May 1961 President John F. Kennedy announced before a special joint session of Congress the dramatic and ambitious goal of sending an American safely to the Moon before the end of the decade. On 20 July 1969, at 20:18, Neil Armstrong and Buzz Aldrin made that ten-year vision a reality. They were the end result, but it was the vision of JFK and the patience and long-time perspective that set the wheels in motion.

The Sistine Chapel took four years for Michelangelo to paint. It took the miniaturist Peter Riches 15 years to complete a dolls' house. The tiny ten-bed mansion, with its own servants' quarters, music room with grand piano, hand-crafted games room with snooker table and library with over 1,000 separately bound books, sold for £50,000. It is estimated that the great pyramid of Giza took two decades to build. It took 50 years to build the Palace of Versailles.

They say it takes 20 years to build a reputation and five minutes to lose it.

So a long-term time perspective – you could call this a long-term view – is mandatory in Life Leverage and getting more done in less time.

If you have to work hard enough not to have to work hard, then for each unit of time you are in a niche or task or enterprise, the inverse relationship between time and money or results swings the other way. At the start you have to 'work' the hardest for the lowest-level, tangible result. It doesn't seem 'fair' but time isn't 'fair' and it is certainly not result-linear. At the 'end' you work the least, the easiest for the highest-level, compounded tangible results. And that doesn't seem fair either.

The flighty, shiny-penny, get-rich-unrealistically-quick mindset is susceptible to believing the opposite of the Law of Compounding. It is the naive belief that somehow, somewhere, you can have little to none of the front-loaded most-of-the-work-for-least-result and almost all the most-of-the-result-with-least-of-the-work, at the start. These people get attracted to something they think can shortcut the Law of Compounding, and, before they've even given the roots a chance to take hold, they give up. They give up and start again and give up and start again and give up and start again, and the only things that compound are pain, misery and low self-worth. Then they get upset, blaming and complaining when it all goes wrong. This is not the Life Leverage philosophy. Ironically, the first thing they started and then stopped may have worked if they had kept at it long enough, even if it wasn't the best thing. Something done at an average level consistently will always beat something done very well for a short time and then given up on.

Depending on your source, here are some interesting comments about the Space Shuttle:

- The Space Shuttle used half its fuel just to get off the ground.

- The Space Shuttle used 96.2 per cent of its fuel to get 30 centimetres into the air.

- The Space Shuttle used nearly all its fuel in the few seconds immediately after launch.

Whichever is statistically correct, you can see the 80/20 Principle and the Law of Compounding in this. Around 80 per cent of the fuel of the Space Shuttle seems to used and needed just to get the shuttle 'off the ground' or to get it going, and around the remaining 20 per cent was used for the entire rest of the voyage out of the atmosphere, into space, and all the way back again.

THE COST OF CHANGE

If more people knew about 80/20 and the Law of Compounding, they would think much more carefully about giving up or changing all the time. They would seriously weigh up continuing what they are doing at a slow and steady pace against looking at the greener grass where it all looks faster, easier and better.

Most people, and especially those who don't succeed, don't give compounding a chance. Most people stop, give up and change course just before the time when compounding kicks in and starts to pay them back. You wouldn't plant a seed, come back the next day and shout 'Where's my tree?' Of course you know that, in order to see the fruits, you've got to grow the roots. If you want to manifest the visible, you've got to master the invisible.

Imagine a constant heads-up display that you could see in your vision, like those you can get on cars as an optional extra, and like computer games. In these you can see 'lives remaining' or 'life force', 'power', 'weapon of choice', 'strengths and weaknesses', 'ammunition remaining' and so on. You have a constant visual measurement in real time of the consequences of your choices and actions. You can see immediately whether you are wasting ammo and energy.

Life doesn't give you one of those, but imagine that it did. Imagine that you had a visual feedback mechanism which showed a power bar or battery-life gauge of your intangible, ethereal progress. Imagine that you could see the bar go up and down according to the future compounded results and consequences of your actions. Imagine the bar four-fifths (80/20) full at the point where it looks like there are little physical results; you'd *never* give up. You'd see the cost of change.

The cost of change is the cost of resetting compounding to zero again. Imagine Tiger Woods giving up golf at 18 years old because he hadn't won a major yet. That would have reset 16 years of time invested, getting him more than 80 per cent of the way towards multiple major wins and entry into golf's Hall of Fame. Even a small swing change can have huge long-term costs, as the best golf coaches know, so should be considered very carefully. Imagine Thomas Edison giving up his experiments for the light bulb on his 9,000th or 9,998th attempt. And there must be so many stories of people who could have gone on to greatness but stopped just before they allowed compounding to start 'reversing' the most-of-the-work-for-least-result with the the most-of-the-result-with-least-of-the-work.

This works with money, time, energy, effort, trees and plants, workflow, exercises at the gym, debt, or your reputation and what you're known for. In fact, it is hard to think about where the Law of Compounding doesn't work, either in acceleration or reverse.

This is not saying you have to work really hard; that is not the Life Leverage way. This is saying that the longer you're in it the less hard you actually have to work for the compounded benefit. It took me around four years from starting a 'real' business to becoming a personal net-worth millionaire, minus all debt. I then made considerably more than a million personally in the next year – more money in less than a quarter of the time it took to make my first million. And it was the 'laziest' of all of the years up to that time, with the least amount of work for the maximum financial results at that time. And so it has continued to compound. I've been told by friends of mine who've made millions, or billions, that this is normal and how it works.

It is the same with your brand and reputation, and what you're known for. When you start a business or enterprise, no one knows you, so no one knows that they can buy from you. You creep forward, one customer at a time, and you don't have the systems, staff or scale to grow fast. You are testing and you're not yet your best, so you're going to be feeling your way in the dark. You don't know how to deal with what lies ahead because you've never been there, so you have to learn the hard way, by making mistakes. You have to get all this out of the way before your first customer will refer you to someone else; just one person, and then it takes more time to build your referral network for the word to spread positively about what you do. Again, you could be almost four-fifths of the way there and starting again resets it all to zero.

We live in a world of instant gratification. We see YouTube videos with 10 million views and get seduced by what seems like overnight successes and celebrities, and before-and-after pictures of six-packs and miracle cures all tempting our desire for shortcuts. This is an unrealistic fantasy that tempts us because we don't have a clear vision, and so we are lured by distractions that look easy from the outside. The long-term reality is poverty, lack of self-worth and fulfilment, because each time you start again, having invested time into growing the roots but seeing no shoots, you have to go through the entire seeding, planting and fertilizing process all over again. The more this happens, the more you lose your confidence in your ability to create compounded success, and you look for further shortcuts to save you because you doubt your own ability. And so the cycle continues.

The deeper the roots, the higher the tree grows towards the sun, the wider and more radiantly its leaves spread, and the more seeds it produces for future forests (generations).

Those 'overnight successes' invested time growing their roots to position themselves for maximum compounding and reach. Those six-packs came from a smart diet, the best exercises performed in perfect form and the best personal trainers to motivate and inspire.

You very often hear people pointing out how the rich get richer and the poor get poorer. Well, this is generally the case because they are attracting more of what they already have, be that wealth and abundance or bills and a scarcity, 'there isn't enough' mentality. You won't attract more wealth until you can learn to manage what you already have.

Compounding gives momentum, and works moving forwards or backwards. Ever-growing percentages of money attract ever-increasing amounts of money. Ever-growing debt attracts ever-increasing amounts of debt.

In fact, the rich have a problem with too much money: they can't reinvest it fast enough, because compounding is compounding on compounding, and because they reinvest it, more money comes in. Yes, the rich do get richer.

Let compounding work for you: don't keep changing all the time and reverse as quickly as possible the front-loaded most-of-the-work-for-least-result at the start to most-of-the-result-with-least-of-the-work the longer you stay in.

Summary

A great quote by Warren Buffett sums up compounding perfectly. When asked by Lewis Howes in his podcast 'The School of Greatness' how he had become so rich, he answered: 'Living in America for the greatest opportunities, having good genes so I lived a long time, and compound interest.' Change has a huge cost. Keep on keeping on, stay patient, learn and grow every day and keep your main thing the main thing.

#10 Overwhelm, confusion and frustration

Overwhelm, confusion and frustration lead to inaction. And they take ages; no other emotions are so slow-cooking and torturous. At least with more significant, painful emotions, it's over fast and you can begin your recovery. The longer you experience overwhelm, frustration and confusion, the less you get done, the longer it takes to get nothing done, and when you finally do make a decision it's nearly always the wrong one because you just want to get rid of the pain.

These three emotions demand their own chapter because they are the most prevalent in blocking decision and action. They are the nemesis of Life Leverage. These three emotions often come together or lead to and from each other. Here's what they are, where they come from, and how to get rid of them.

OVERWHELM

Overwhelm is an often self-induced feeling of being completely overcome in mind and emotion. Ironically, one definition of overwhelm is 'to cover or bury beneath something'. That is how you feel when you are overwhelmed.

You feel overwhelmed when you have too many things to do and not enough time to do them. You feel overwhelmed when you are doing too many things for other people with imposed actions and deadlines. You feel overwhelmed when you can't handle the pace of tasks or your brain can't handle the amount or speed of learning. You feel overwhelmed when you are being pressured to do too many things that aren't important to you or when you can't see an end to them. You feel overwhelmed when you feel out of control of your tasks, time or life. You might even feel overwhelmed reading this paragraph on overwhelm!

Most people find it hard to get rid of overwhelm. That's not surprising because you can't see what you can't see, you don't know what you don't know, and if you knew how to get rid of it, you'd have got rid of it already. Many people try to write it all down, but if you write down everything on your to-do list you may feel overwhelmed just looking at it! Writing it down does dump it out of your head, which can be a cathartic process, but it takes a lot more than that to actually banish it.

Here is a simple five-step system to quickly and with minimal effort banish overwhelm:

Step 1. Take full and personal responsibility.

Step 2. Check your vision (V), values (V) and KRAs (K).

Step 3. Drop, let go of and say 'No' to anything that is not a KRA (K) or an IGT (I).

Step 4. Prioritize according to the highest KRA (K) and IGT (I).

Step 5. Focus single-mindedly on the most important, first task only.

Let's look at each of these steps in a little more detail:

Step 1. Take full and personal responsibility.

Never blame, complain or justify. Be careful what you wish for, because everything you have to do in your life, you allowed in. It's no one else's fault that you're doing too many things, or doing something that you don't want to do, or that you're in way too deep and your brain is deep-fat-fried. Once you've got over yourself and stopped blaming the world for your overwhelm, you can take back control and do something about it.

Step 2. Check your vision (V), values (V) and KRAs (K).

The cure to virtually all overwhelm, confusion and frustration is to go back to doing what most inspires you according to your highest vision and values. No one will feel overwhelmed if they have too much of what they love to do the most, or too much of living their vision and legacy. If you feel overwhelmed, it's likely that you've got distracted away from your vision and values, so check back in, remind yourself of what most inspires you, your purpose and your highest values and priorities, and now you have a KRA and an IGT game plan to focus on.

Step 3. Drop, let go of and say 'No' to anything that is not a KRA (K) or an IGT (I).

You must be ruthless and drop, let go of and say 'No' to anything demanding your time and occupying your mind that isn't a KRA or an IGT. It is all those tasks that are urgent emergencies to other people but not high priority or in line with your vision, dumped on you, which are causing your overwhelm. It is the weight of responsibility you feel, the guilt of not helping, added to the unconscious knowledge that this isn't progressing you.

> 'When things aren't adding up in your life, start subtracting.'
> – Anon.

You have to delegate or dump those low-KRA and -IGT tasks. And when you have done this, you mustn't let more back in. People who are in a constant state of overwhelm, blaming external factors, don't see their unconscious behaviour. They drop, delegate or completely dump tasks, only to fill the gap again. It's like trying to empty a bucket without turning off the tap.

What behaviour or mindset is causing you to maintain overwhelm?

Think about these questions carefully:

- Do you have a false sense of responsibility to others?

- Do your vision and values lack clarity?

- Are you unable to or find it difficult to say 'No'?

- Do you find yourself helping people and then getting stuck because you have bitten off more than you can chew, or do you find you can't get your own things done so you start to feel frustrated and resentful?

- Are you unrealistic about what you can and can't get done?

- Is that because you are unrealistic about how long things take?

- Are you a bit over-ambitious?

- Are you scared of losing or missing out on something?

- Do you want people to think you are superhuman?

Whatever it is that's causing you to feel overwhelmed, identify it, be honest with yourself and *let it go*.

Step 4. Prioritize according to the highest KRA (K) and IGT (I).

Once you have gained a moment of clarity on your values and vision, and you've delegated or dumped *all* tasks not in line with your vision and values, you then need to prioritize them strictly according to your Key Result Areas (KRAs) that deliver your vision and values, and then list them in ruthless order of highest priority and/or income generation. You start with the highest KRAs possible, and then order them according to the highest IGT where it's not clear if one KRA is higher than the other. Don't worry: in the next section we will look at VVKIK in detail and how you do this will become clear.

Step 5. Focus single-mindedly on the most important, first task only.

The acronym FOCUS stands for 'Follow One Course Until Successful'. Do not move on to No.2 until No.1 is completely done. Simple system, right? Ha, if only. Remember that the definition of discipline is doing what you know you have to do, whether you feel like it or not. Think of how great you will feel after you have completed your important task. Make sure that you're held accountable by someone who won't let you off the hook. Give yourself a reward afterwards. Isolate yourself from all potential distractions. Do whatever it takes.

CONFUSION

Confusion is actually very simple. There are many words and phrases people use or that the dictionary comes up with, but it can be summed up in three words: lack of clarity. If you have a lack of clarity in any area of your life, of course you are going to be confused. Confusion can come from a lack of knowledge or experience, too many options and an inability to decide or prioritize. It can come from doubt in yourself and your (in)ability to implement something effectively, or from feeling that you don't know the best or right way of deciding or doing something. Confusion can lead to overwhelm or come as a result of overwhelm. As confusion is linked to overwhelm, if you follow the five-step process to banishing overwhelm, confusion will turn to clarity.

If you want an additional quick, surefire way of banishing confusion, follow the simple steps below:

Step 1. Check your vision (V), values (V) and KRAs (K).

Step 2. Drop, let go of and say 'No' to any non-KRAs (K) or -IGTs (I).

Step 3. Prioritize according to the highest KRA (K) and IGT (I).

Step 4. Decide fast, now, and take immediate action on the first task.

There's no need to go over Steps 1 to 3 again; you can reread them if you need to. The slight distinction in Step 4 is the speed of decision and action. Because confusion is a void state, where you are not deciding

'Yes' or 'No', not moving forwards or even backwards to move forwards, you stay stuck, lost and in a void that goes nowhere but takes a long time to get there.

So you must decide fast, as soon as you have gone through Steps 1 to 3.

It's not that important if the task you do is the right task for the long term, but it's important that you get traction to get out of the void and moving in a direction with some velocity. If you end up making the wrong decision, at least you got moving, even if it was backwards at first, and you give yourself the chance to get feedback to tweak and alter the course as you go.

FRUSTRATION

Frustration is, according to one dictionary definition, a 'feeling of dissatisfaction, often accompanied by anxiety or depression, resulting from unfulfilled needs or unresolved problems'. It's blindingly obvious that frustration doesn't come from doing what you love and loving what you do, living to your highest values and vision, and doing the tasks that get you there. So there's the epiphany, right? Again, if only it were that easy ...

If you are (mostly) doing what you love, then you will endure 'the struggle'. You will accept frustration as part of the journey; sometimes you will even enjoy the 'struggle' because you intuitively know it's the right course of action. Mohammad Ali endured the hours of training and Thomas Edison endured all the failed experiments because they knew they were on their path of spontaneous right action towards a worthwhile vision that gave them purpose. Sure, you're going to get frustrated, but you understand what it is and that it is fleeting.

Frustration is often the result of overwhelm and confusion. It is what you do to yourself after you've done overwhelm and confusion to yourself.

Here are the steps to banish frustration:

Step 1. Stop beating yourself up.

Step 2. What is the 'feedback' telling you?

Step 3. Check your vision (V), values (V) and KRAs (K), as above.

Step 4. Prioritize according to highest KRA (K) and IGT (I), as above.

Step 5. Focus single-mindedly on the most important, first task only (as above).

Step 6. Allow yourself reward, celebration and to feel good.

Let's look at the steps in more detail.

Step 1. Stop beating yourself up.

The more you get frustrated at yourself for being frustrated, the more you get frustrated. It's a vicious cycle. The best thing you can do for yourself is stop beating yourself up and compounding the misery, stop feeling sorry for or annoyed with yourself, and take forward action to get rid of it.

You are not your frustration. You are not the feelings you're feeling; they are just feelings.

Do not let your feelings of frustration damage your self-esteem or belief in yourself. Understand them for what they are: feedback mechanisms to tweak, change and grow. In another day, week, month or year these feelings will have completely gone and you will have grown and moved to a higher level. At this higher level, the older feelings of frustration will no longer bother you. It will only be higher-level problems that will induce these feelings.

Step 2. What is the 'feedback' telling you?

The feeling of frustration is feedback that you aren't doing the right things, or the right things in the right way. So it's actually a very positive feeling to feel, because it is a fair-warning sign that you are not living or acting congruently with your highest values and vision. You therefore need to give up on it, or if you are clear that it is the right thing to do, it is feedback that you need to do it more, better or differently, and you need to improve to move to the higher level of growth.

Either way, you need to 'listen' to your frustration and 'see' it for what it is, 'identifying' the changes you need to make. Expecting a different result from doing more of the same thing is delusional.

Step 3. Check your vision (V), values (V) and KRAs (K).

We've already covered this in this chapter. Please go back to the section on overwhelm, Step 2, if you need a reminder.

Step 4. Prioritize according to highest KRA (K) and IGT (I).

We've already covered this in this chapter. Please go back to the section on overwhelm, Step 4, if you need a reminder.

Step 5. Focus single-mindedly on the most important, first task only.

We've already covered this in this chapter. Please go back to the section on overwhelm, Step 5, if you need a reminder.

Step 6. Allow yourself reward, celebration and to feel good.

Once you have gained clarity, taken personal responsibility and proactively banished frustration, then you have mastered your emotions and shown a level of self-control and understanding most people will never achieve. You should pat yourself on the back for this; you're amazing. You're a unique genius and you apply your wisdom. Celebrate. Reward yourself. Anchor those positive feelings and successes, no matter how small, because you will form new habits and create momentum. All small wins lead to big wins.

To constantly go from task to task and goal to goal without celebrating or rewarding yourself is self-defeating, because you are always looking for the next and biggest achievement to feel happy and contented, but as soon as you get there you are addicted to needing the next thing, which is always elusive because it becomes the next thing and the next thing and the next thing. Too much materialism or keeping up with the Joneses can leave you feeling empty and unfulfilled, despite so many successes and lessons and despite your growth along the way.

The Life Leverage way of dealing with overwhelm, confusion and frustration is:

1. Understand what the feelings are/mean and that you caused them

2. Take the necessary feedback and understand that you can make changes to control this

3. Follow the Life Leverage models and systems to banish them.

Summary

Overwhelm, confusion and frustration are some of the biggest blocks to Life Leverage. Start now and focus on one high KRA/IGT at a time. Get perfect later. Compartmentalize your time and isolate yourself from all distractions and devices. Drop tasks that are low on your values or a low IGT, say 'No' more often and disregard other people's opinions and urgencies when they try to impose them on you.

Section 2: Strategy

The reason many people don't succeed in controlling and managing their life on their terms isn't because they can't, it's because they don't know what 'life on their terms' actually looks like. They haven't defined their vision, and then employed the right strategies to deliver that vision. They haven't set the course to navigate towards. You wouldn't get in a car and just drive. You'd want to know where the destination is before you drive, know how to follow the shortest possible route, missing the accidents, incidents and traffic jams, being guided each step of the way. If you just drive, you'll spend a lot of time and burn a lot of fuel going nowhere in particular. And that's how most people are living their life or running their enterprises.

The first chapter in this section looks at **VVKIK**, which stands for:

- **Vision (V)**

- **Values (V)**

- **KRAs (K)**

- **IGTs (I)**

- **KPIs (K).**

In that order, these are the guaranteed ways of gaining clarity in your life and intuitively and spontaneously knowing the right thing to do in the right moment, and therefore the right thing to do in every moment. The entire Life Leverage philosophy and every system, model and technique are built around and based upon the fundamental architecture of VVKIK.

Strategy is more about thinking than doing. The reason most overwhelmingly busy or poor people spend more time doing than thinking is because they think doing more leads to results and money. They link hard work with results. They think the best thing they can do is just crack on and work hard, getting the jobs done and moving on to the next ones.

Running faster and harder the wrong way is the wrong way, yet most people are on that never-ending treadmill.

Strategy is thinking time to create the right vision, direction and plan of action for you and your enterprise.

Strategy is the constant checking in that the tasks and systems are in tune with your vision, operating correctly and in highest order of priority.

Most people forget why they even started their business in the first place, and end up being a slave to the very thing they used to be so passionate about. They become task-junkies and drop business planning and vision because they are just too busy.

It is the higher vision that keeps you going when there are challenges or difficulties and it seems that you're not progressing. It is the strategic time that keeps you checking in, evaluating and reporting between vision and operation.

In golf, you are allowed to play with 14 golf clubs. Conventional, non-Life Leverage, non-strategic thinking would therefore be to practise equally with each club. Beat as many balls as you can down the range without thinking about it, rotating from club to club.

Wrong. Statistically, up to 65 per cent of shots taken in a round of golf are from 100 yards or less. You need between two and four clubs of the 14 available for shots within 100 yards. So, on rough average, 65 per cent of the shots a professional takes is with three of the 14 clubs available, or 21 per cent.

Just as interesting, statistically, is that up to 40 per cent of shots taken in a round of golf are with the putter. So roughly 40 per cent of the shots are taken with one club, or 7.14 per cent of the clubs available.

So will it pay to divide your practice time equally between clubs? Absolutely not. If you apply Life Leverage philosophy and thinking, you are better off practising the most with the putter, the next most with the short-range clubs, and the rest with the rest. You are best off practising least with the club that you will use the least.

We could go much deeper into this, strategically, should it be relevant. We could analyse what shot gets you into trouble the most and costs the most shots, so you practise avoiding that. We could analyse the right courses to play on that are most likely to host the relevant competitions you would enter. We could analyse how knowing yardage and major hazards could be studied and negated. But that's for a different book.

What is for this book is the process; the strategic thinking that creates 80/20, Life Leverage results.

This next section details the strategic aspects of Life Leverage to guide you towards getting more done in less time, outsourcing everything and living your ideal mobile life

#11 VVKIK

How do you know if what you're doing is the right thing? Are you moving towards your vision and legacy? Do you even know what they are? Do you ever feel overwhelmed, frustrated or experience procrastination, fear of making mistakes or doubt about the right action?

Most people start at the wrong place – at the bottom. They do more, work harder, stay busy on unimportant tasks to trick themselves into feeling productive. Their boss, their 'guru' and their conscience tell them to work hard, hard, hard and harder. They dig faster and deeper in the wrong direction.

To check in on your progress and productivity, start at the top of the VVKIK architecture explained below. Check the list of Life Leverage vitals and check that you know/are doing them, then your actions will naturally and spontaneously be right for maximum inspiration and results. The higher up the VVKIK you work, the more the ones below them fall into place with least effort, and the more intuitively you can decide with more haste, volition and less risk on your next action, moment to moment.

VALUES (V)

Values are the things that are most important to you in your life, in order of priority. Your values are unique to you. No one else on the planet has exactly the same values as you in the same order of priority, because if two people on the planet were the same, one wouldn't be needed. You are an inspired genius in being you, because no one else is like you, and when you are authentic you are the best you that anyone else could be. It's not that you're better or worse than anyone else, because everyone is unique, but you are a better you than anyone else on the planet.

The problem is that most people don't really know who they are, at least not consciously. They are not authentic and they don't honour their values. The first step in honouring your values is thus knowing what they are.

The following exercise will give you multiple epiphanies, clarity and focus. It will help you value yourself more and stop self-defeating emotions and delusions. It will order your life and your actions for intuitive and spontaneous clarity. It is the bedrock on which the Life Leverage philosophy is built.

Warning: this exercise will change your life.

So be prepared now for your life to change. Take the time to do this exercise properly and completely. Isolate yourself from distractions and do the following:

1. Write down on paper or your device what you feel is most important to you in your life.

2. Consider higher levels of abstraction and concept such as health, family, wealth, freedom, happiness, learning, success, growth, travel, appearance and so on.

3. Keep going until you run out of words or you look at the concepts and don't feel inspired by them.

4. Evaluate the list carefully, then reorder it according to what you want to change in your life, for example moving money or family up the list.

To help you with this process, consider the following:

1. What do you spend most of your time doing?

2. What could you love doing all day long without external pressure?

3. What do you fill your space with (home, office, car, etc.)?

4. What do you think about consistently?

5. What are you most known for?

6. Where do results already show and not show in your life (whether you like them or not)?

Try not to trick or second-guess yourself in this exercise by what you think you should think, or what you say to others, or what you want for the future you. If you are an amazing cook at home or you are one of the best you know at computer games or you have 14 dozen hand-bags, then that is what it is. Honour the process and do it without judgement, let it flow and enjoy the process. It is important that you do this now, even if you are listening to Life Leverage on audio. Pause me and take some time to do this exercise.

Assuming you have done this, now you have a list to look at that represents you, a mirror of you, your life's guide and what governs every action you take. Imagine if you had done this at school. Imagine if you knew the blueprint that governed and masterminded your own life. Imagine if you redid this every year or six months of your life to check and adjust and re-coordinate. But this exercise isn't about dwelling in the past, it is about moving forward, fast. It is vital that you have your list of life's values with you at all times on your device or on the cloud or in your notebook. You are going through the process of making the unconscious conscious, the invisible visible, and you will need constant reminders while it is new.

One of the very best ways to make your values go from unconscious to conscious and invisible to visible is to read your list of values immediately before you go to bed, and immediately as you wake. It will take two minutes to read the list two or three times and consider them, just four minutes a day. Within just a few weeks you will know these unconsciously and intuitively, and your actions will start to mirror your values, in what you do and also what you drop.

Your unconscious mind does not sleep as your conscious mind does. You know that because you wake up and all the vital signs that keep you alive clearly worked, and you may have had vivid dreams, too. You know that often you dream about things that happened during the day, or strong emotions you felt in reaction to a situation just before you went to bed. So clearly what you think about comes about in your unconscious mind. So you now have the opportunity to control that.

The science behind this relates to two factors:

1. Emotion

2. Repetition (anchoring).

1. Emotion

Emotion is a key factor in how your subconscious mind digests information, so the more emotional the experience the more impactful the memory. Your mind does not know the difference between real and imagined content (this is why dreams feel real at the time), so whatever you want your mind to help you accomplish, say it out loud and say it with emotion. The more emotion you use, the better results you will get, because it will be real to your unconscious mind. Imagine your values as real, now, and imagine yourself living them out with passion, freedom and happiness.

2. Repetition

The other part of getting the best results from your subconscious mind is that you need to use the magic of message repetition to form habits that move you from consciously incompetent to unconsciously competent. Remember trying to ride your bike or driving a car for the first time?

Condition your unconscious mind while you are awake during the day and asleep at night to create unconscious habits for achieving and intuitively knowing the things you want to master.

There is a story/legend of US Navy pilot Captain Jack Sands. He was a pilot who was shot down during the Vietnam War and captured. He became a prisoner of war (POW) and spent seven years in Hanoi, at the prison camp famously known as the Hanoi Hilton. Captain Sands, like other POWs, was kept in absolute isolation. No physical activity was permitted and human contact was limited. He 'lived' in solitary confinement in a 1.5-metre-square cage for seven years.

Although he was confined physically, he realized that he didn't have to be confined mentally. He started the process in his mind of constructing a perfect golf course. He created this image in every detail, including all the sights, smells and feelings. He imagined the grass, the trees, even the clothes on his back, and created a mental image of each of the 18 holes. Then he set out to play the course.

Every day for seven years Captain Sands set foot on that golf course and played 18 holes, stroke by stroke. He experienced, in his mind, the wind, sounds, smells, and how it felt to make each of those swings at the ball. And since this was his course, and his game, he hit every stroke perfectly. Each swing was perfect, each approach shot was perfect, and each putt was perfect. Captain Sands had the luxury in that 1.5-square-metre box of enjoying a perfect round of golf every day.

Captain Sands was a casual golfer before he became a Navy pilot, occasionally playing the game and always shooting around 100. After seven years of perfect mental golf, however, things changed. Once he was released and made it back home, Captain Sands scored a 74 on the first round he played in over eight years. Not only had he not played a round of golf; he had had no physical activity under the harshest of treatment and conditions, yet he shaved over 20 strokes off his game.

The lesson of this story is that reality is largely formed in your mind. Superstars in any activity expect to win, regardless of the conditions or the situation. It is that expectation that sets their course and results in superior performance. And it's something that you can use in your life, in whatever you do.

This isn't just positive thinking; this is creating the full 'video' in your mind in exacting detail, from start to finish, and replaying it over and over. It's not doing it one time or every once in a while. It's taking time each day to do it until it becomes your mental reality. That mental reality will transform the actual one. It seems simple in concept, but very few of us will take the time, every day, to do this.

You can research this story and, like many surprising stories that have become legends, you will find that there are different versions. You can choose to believe it or not. If you think you can, or you think you can't, you're right. But imagine for a moment if you just spent those four minutes, before bed and before you get out of bed, every day, using this same process to programme your values into your unconscious mind. What could your amazing mind attract into your life, given the chance?

As you look at your list of values, you are able to see your passions and pains, vacations and vocations, what you are inspired by and what you need to be motivated for, right in front of your very eyes. Right up until this moment, you have been unconsciously drawn to and focused on those highest on the list, and away from those lowest or not on the list, and most likely in the order and hierarchy in which they appear.

If you don't like what you see, and/or you want your life to change, then make a conscious decision to reorder your values. Your values will, and can, change through your life, either organically over time (for example, health usually moves up the older you get), because of a significant emotional event that was strong enough to force change, or through a conscious decision to change. If you want to make a change in your life, the deepest root of change and the most likely to create fast and lasting change is a values change, because values drive everything you do in your life.

Values most often come from voids, because we make important in life what we haven't achieved or received yet. Someone who feels they have enough money will no longer see it as important to them, because they have filled the void, and so something will naturally usurp its rank in your values hierarchy. This is why yo-yo dieters yo-yo, because their diet is more important to them the worse their diet and body are, where the pain is the highest. But as soon as the diet is good or the weight is gone, the pain has gone, and the ice cream comes back into play. We have all known how motivated we can be to diet like mad before a big event in order to fit into a particular outfit, only to 'relax' health- and diet-wise afterwards and put the weight back on. It is only when a new motivation arises that we may feel inspired to get in better shape, so health will become a priority again. When our confidence drops as a consequence of criticism (or unfavourable comparison!), the impact on our health and well-being can be considerable and become a permanent fixture in our values hierarchy.

The point of these examples is to show how values drive your life. Most people only scratch the surface of control and change in their lives, because they work only on superficial tasks and tactics. The deeper your overwhelm, confusion and frustration (which can lead to anxiety and depression), the more important it is to look deeper into your values.

When you feel these three emotions, ask yourself 'Are my actions in line with what is most important to me in my life?' You will naturally know, because this is where you naturally spend the most time, are in the state of flow, where time flies, and your results show. If you are out of that state, either you aren't functioning in line with your values or you haven't linked how this short-term pain links to or serves your highest values. So to get back to an inspired state, either make your action/focus/vocation important to you or link the short-term action to how it serves your highest values, and you will follow through with the task, no matter how easy or challenging it is in the transient moment. It also helps you to know what you should give up on and focus more on.

VISION (V)

Do you have a clear picture and outcome of the purpose you want your life to serve? The legacy you want to leave? How you want to be remembered? The difference you want to make on this planet? These are important questions that most people usually don't take the time to answer.

Your vision is the ultimate manifestation of your values, lived with inspiration. Your vision is the roadmap for your life guiding you in each moment through crossroads, tough choices, setbacks, diversions and transient periods where you lack clarity and experience confusion.

Most people on the planet don't have a true 'vision', which explains why most people don't feel a sense of purpose, inspiration or achievement. If you don't know what you want or what your destination looks like, you're never going to get there. A vision could also be seen as a purpose, and living a life *of* purpose means living life *on* purpose.

Without a vision and purpose, you have no purpose. If a human being serves no purpose, they become irrelevant to the evolution and survival of the species. This goes some way to explaining why so many people wrestle through their lives looking for the meaning of life. I believe the meaning of life is to find your true, unique purpose, so that you add value to humanity and therefore help evolve our species.

> *'The purpose of life is a life of purpose.'*
> – Robin Sharma

This also goes some way to explaining why those with a bigger, clearer vision grow, become successful, help to evolve the human race and leave legacies that inspire others, while those with no vision, direction or purpose often feel empty, depressed and sometimes even resort to suicide. No one with sound mental faculties and a clear vision and purpose ever took their own life.

In the UK, research by the NHS (National Health Service) has shown that many people who die by suicide have a mental illness, most commonly depression or an alcohol problem. In many cases, suicide is also linked to feelings of hopelessness and worthlessness. So, assuming that all mental faculties are in place, a lack of hope and self-worth, translated to a lack of vision and purpose, is one of the biggest causes of suicide.

Sudden lack of purpose also creates 'Broken Heart Syndrome', discussed earlier, where people who retire or lose a loved one can – in what seems to be randomly and without warning – just die through strong and sudden anxiety and stress that physically swells the heart.

So vision and purpose really are life's driving force. I'm saddened by the fact that I was taught 'Géographie' in school (see Introduction), while an important subject such as 'How to live a life of meaning' is never even touched upon.

In his moving book *Man's Search for Meaning*, Viktor Frankl, an Austrian existential psychologist, created a school of thought called logotherapy. Unlike Sigmund Freud, who said our main motivations are sex and aggression, Frankl surmised that our dominant driving force is to find meaning in life.

Frankl experienced something that Freud never had. In the 1940s Frankl was held prisoner in Nazi concentration camps. Frankl lived that reality. He felt the horror of losing everything, only to be tortured and terrorized. With all the agony and brutality, what kept Frankl from giving up his relentless fight for his life was purpose. He found meaning in his struggle, and that's what gave him the power to push forward through unimaginable pain.

After escaping the concentration camps, Frankl published *Man's Search for Meaning*, which explores his experiences and gives an overview of logotherapy. A quote by Friedrich Nietzsche nicely sums up Frankl's philosophy on how people were able to survive the camps, without losing the will to live:

'He who has a why to live for can bear almost any how.'
– Friedrich Nietzsche

That is the power of purpose and vision – even the most unimaginable inhumanity and torture can be beaten by vision and purpose. Purpose is what gives us the strength to carry on, if not through dire conditions, then through difficult challenges, transitions, relationships and activities. Purpose gives us clarity, focus and hope that things will be bigger and better.

'In some ways suffering ceases to be
suffering at the moment it finds a meaning.'
– Viktor Frankl

Do you think now is a good time to create your vision that allows you to live your values and a higher purpose? This is a big thing, though; it's not like choosing your shopping list. This is your life.

Let's have fun and play a game. Here are some examples of visions of well-known companies and individuals. Can you guess whose visions they are?

1. To organize the world's information and make it universally accessible and useful

2. To build a place where people can come to find and discover anything they might want to buy online.

3. To change the way the world moves

4. Global eradication of polio

5. To become wealthy

6. Exceedingly good cakes

7. Global financial freedom

OK, no cheating, as the answers are coming. How did you do? My guess is that you'll know three.

Here are the answers:

1. Google

2. Amazon

3. Ford

4. Bill & Melinda Gates Foundation

5. Warren Buffett

6. Mr Kipling

7. Progressive Property (one of my companies; OK, not so well known as the others!)

While these visions are different from one another, the one thing all these people and companies have in common is crystal clarity of purpose. Their vision is BIG. It is bigger than they are. It has to be if it is going to keep them going, experiencing happiness and sadness along the way, as they engage with the never-ending pursuit of a worthy life and legacy. Vision gives you direction, it creates a leader in you that guides others, and it creates spontaneous inspiration through all emotions. Vision changes the world and helps the human race evolve.

So ask yourself these questions, and get down on paper or on your device some thoughts about your vision and purpose. Start now. Get perfect later. It will evolve, so don't procrastinate because you don't think you are worthy of a big vision, or you don't know, or you think it's hard; just get some thoughts out of your head now:

- What purpose does your life serve?

- What is the vision of your life that will serve others and outlive you?

- Why is it so important to you?

- What do you want your life to look like in three, five, ten, 25, 50 years?

- How do you want to be remembered?

Once you have sketched out some answers to these questions, you can regularly check back on your vision to remove overwhelm, confusion and frustration immediately.

People and companies with a clear and larger-than-themselves vision know intuitively and spontaneously what they want. Some call this the law of attraction, some the power of focus; others call it manifestation.

Call it what you will, it works. And it really doesn't matter what it is, or how big it is, as long as you're happy with it, it will give you the inspiration and self-drive to live your life, on your terms, with authenticity and meaning, and in a way that serves others, too.

Don't compare yourself to anyone else other than for inspiration, or worry about what friends, family or society project on to you; just think about *you*. After all, if you are the best you that you can be, you will serve others the best as a result.

Don't skip this step. Take the time to seriously think about these questions. This is the first step to the rest of your life, and you deserve it.

Once you have considered your vision, you can link your vision with your values. How do your values serve your vision and help you get ever closer to it? Make sure they are aligned. There's no point saying you want to be on the rich list when wealth isn't even in your top ten values. So take time now to align your vision with your values, tweaking and reordering where appropriate.

If you want some help, or you want to share them with like-minded individuals, or you want to be held accountable to them, you can 'like' the following page and share them on my wall.

www.facebook.com/robmooreprogressive

Let me know what you think of the book so far, and share your vision and values. If you tag me in, I can help you or give you feedback if you want it.

KEY RESULT AREAS (KRAs)

Key Result Areas are the highest-value areas that you focus on to achieve your vision. KRAs are the three to seven areas in which you should invest most of your time to make the maximum difference to your team, your company and your legacy.

KRAs are often strategic, leveraged tasks and functions such as developing and maintaining relationships, building an amazing network/ mastermind, developing systems, raising finance, business planning and strategy, board meetings, constant self-education, and so on.

If you get stuck or dragged into micro day-to-day tasks, you have probably lost focus of your KRAs, because detailed, operational and practical tasks are mostly not KRAs, they are *tasks*. If you feel overwhelmed, confused or frustrated, you have probably been dragged into someone else's KRAs. It's that feeling you have where you have 'worked' all day but got no real 'work' done – well, at least not work that meant something to you.

On a daily, weekly, monthly, six-monthly and yearly basis, at the very least, check against your KRAs that you are performing functions of the highest importance that make the biggest different to achieving your vision and living according to your highest values.

Check to-do lists, tasks and requests by others against your KRAs. If it serves them, do it; if it doesn't, delegate or dump it. Be ruthless. KRAs give clarity. KRAs give you the shortest possible route to the best possible outcome towards your goals and vision. KRAs instantly remove overwhelm and frustration and get your endorphins flowing, because you intuitively know you are taking the single right action.

Progress, momentum and compounding make you feel good and build your sense of self-worth and ability to achieve more.

If you have staff or you hire people, you must create KRAs for their role. Here are some of the main complaints of employees at work that cause them to hate or leave their job:

- I don't feel appreciated.

- I have no clear purpose (personally or for the company).

- I don't feel I make a difference.

- My boss doesn't care about me.

- Job expectations are unrealistic.

- I have too many projects at once.

At least four of them, and, it could be argued, all of them, are related to KRAs. Your staff/team need clarity. They need to have a clear purpose in their role that is linked to a clear purpose in your enterprise. They need to know what they are supposed to do that gives them the right expectations to deliver, knowing that the task has high value, that it makes a difference, and what to prioritize. If they are performing the highest-value functions they can for their career and your enterprise, they will feel that they are making a difference (because they are performing at the very highest level they can) and will therefore feel valued and inspired.

The KRAs for your team member, and for you, should be on the job description, at the top. Forget reams of tasks and operations; write out the role in one clear paragraph, and then immediately underneath list the three to seven KRAs to perform that role. These are the mandatory requirements to fulfil the role, and they also give a clear guideline on how to deliver maximum benefit and satisfaction to the individual and the enterprise.

In your goals/vision document that you keep with you at all times, you should have your KRAs near the top, under your vision and legacy. Later in *Life Leverage* I will share with you a gift that has this all in one place.

INCOME-GENERATING TASKS (IGTs)

Income-generating tasks are tasks of the highest value to you (or your company) that align with and serve your KRAs. IGTs leverage your highest possible financial value and maximize revenue per hour, minute and second. IGTs are the tasks that bring the highest, leveraged results directly related to income, in the optimum amount of time, bringing maximum benefit and minimum wastage. IGTs get more done and more earned in less time.

Overwhelm, confusion and frustration in your ever-growing to-do list comes from lack of focus on IGTs, giving equal importance to all tasks, or lacking order of IGT priority. All tasks are *not* equal. As mentioned before, in golf, 40 per cent of the shots most professionals take are with 7.14 per cent of the available clubs (the putter). Spending more time and more priority on putting practice will increase a golfer's scores the most, in the shortest, most leveraged use of time. And so it is with focusing on IGTs in highest order and priority to bring in maximum revenue in the shortest time frame, freeing up the majority of time to either do more IGTs or more of what you love that isn't 'work'.

Later in *Life Leverage* you will work out what your current income-generating value (IGV) is worth to the nearest pound or dollar, and you will learn a simple algorithm that will help you multiply it by a factor of 16 almost immediately.

KEY PERFORMANCE INDICATORS (KPIs)

Key Performance Indicators are the important, non-vanity metrics of your business, enterprise and personal goals that keep it moving forward, reduce mistakes and optimize leverage.

You can't master what you don't measure.

KPIs are the vital data sets that tell you in as real time as possible exactly what is happening, or failing, in your business. KPIs become more and more vital as you grow, hand over control and become more removed / more strategic.

The most common mistake is setting up your KPIs too late, or not at all, because they take time, and take time away from urgent, more functional tasks. But that's like not eating because you are too busy working, not learning because you are too busy doing, or not taking the cheque to cash in at the bank because you are too busy working.

KPIs serve your KRAs, because they give real-time feedback that operating your KRAs and IGTs are giving the right outcome, or not. You can test, tweak or change your KRAs and IGTs when you get feedback through KPIs. Because you don't know what you don't know, if you don't have KPIs, you could just as likely and easily be doing the wrong thing, going in the wrong direction, and working really hard to get there/nowhere.

Imagine if you had no sales metrics/KPIs in a sales organization. You could be selling lots of something that makes a net loss, not knowing any different. It would be utterly self-defeating, even a touch insane, to do more and more of what is not working, yet it is probably fair to say that most small businesses aren't systemized enough with enough real-time KPI data. Is it therefore any surprise that up to nine in ten of businesses set up fail in the first year, and then up to eight in ten of those in the next three years?

Start compiling your KPIs now, personally and for your business. Start with the ones that come to mind, such as goals you set that you check in against, metrics for your sales, marketing and financial reporting. Do not use the excuse that you do not know what your KPIs should be, because you could easily come up with the main ones by taking a little time to consider them. You run your life and your enterprise, so you will know the most important ones intuitively.

From there, here are some ways to become more systemized and less operational, to get more done in less time, to outsource everything and create your ideal mobile lifestyle:

1. Read books on data/business growth.

2. Ask bigger business owners what they measure.

3. Troubleshoot your business; look to solve problems.

4. Analyse your existing KPIs.

5. Survey your team and your customers.

Let's look at each one.

1. Read books on data/business growth.

I personally got a lot out of Mark Homer's *Low Cost Life*, Verne Harnish's *Scaling Up*, John Warrollow and Bo Burlingham's *Built to Sell*, Les McKeown's *Predictable Success*, Charles Burck and Larry Bossidy's *Execution: The discipline of getting things done*, Jim Collins and Morten T. Hansen's *Great by Choice*, Terry Leahy's *Management in Ten Words* and Josh Kaufman's *The Personal MBA*. These, while not all specifically about listing KPIs, will give you a great set of metrics if you learn and implement what you read in them.

2. Ask bigger business owners what they measure.

They've been there before, and had and solved the problems you are having or not measuring. Ask them what they do/measure, then implement immediately all relevant ones.

3. Troubleshoot your business; look to solve problems.

If you ask the right questions, you get the right answers. Look to solve the problems of your life and business, and you will unearth what you need to measure so that it doesn't happen again.

4. Analyse your existing KPIs.

Reading and thinking about your current metrics will spark off ideas about new ones. Failing KPIs will create new niche KPIs that are needed to give you overall data that is valuable. Low staff morale, sickness and absenteeism may be linked to it, or retention rates as a percentage of overall staff, or retention rates broken down into left versus fired versus retired.

5. Survey your team and your customers.

Ask your team and your customers what the most important parts of the business are. What are the bottlenecks? What information do they not have access to? What should we start, stop and keep? You'll find all the answers you need, hidden right in front of you.

CONCLUSION

You now have a cyclical feedback loop to constantly stay on track, to be more 'in flow' and less 'on the go' from your highest unique values through to the micro-metrics, and back up again. You have a system and a hierarchy that give clarity and direction, enabling you to do the things that matter the most to you, serve the most people and manifest your unique legacy. You deserve to spend time on yourself, so get some quiet time away from the humdrum, isolate yourself from white noise, and work from the top down. A little KRA and IGT investment on this and you will see your life take a course that makes the biggest difference, gives instant fulfilment and fills you with gratitude.

Summary

The entire Life Leverage philosophy is based upon the fundamental architecture of VVKIK: Vision, Values, Key Result Areas, Income-Generating Tasks and Key Performance Indicators. You will live a life you love if you focus on and continually evaluate your progress against your VVKIKs. Clarity, vision, legacy, wealth and freedom all come from your VVKIKs. Spend strategic, uninterrupted time discovering, developing and progressing them and evaluate them at least every six months.

#12 Serving and solving

As a human race, we serve no purpose if we have no value. We literally get evolved out of the species; it's survival of the fittest. When people lose purpose completely they wither and, as NHS research has shown, sometimes end their own life. You will never find two human beings with the same DNA blueprint, fingerprints or set of values. If two people on the planet are exactly the same, one isn't needed.

The way to have unique value to the human race is to 'serve and solve'. The way you help your species to survive, thrive and evolve is to support its evolution, adding value and service to its collaborative progression. The more value you add, the more valuable you become as a part of the greater whole, and the more reliant the greater whole is on you for evolution and progression.

Translated into your life, and the Life Leverage philosophy, the more you serve others, the more problems you solve for others and the bigger the problems you solve for others, the more you add value to your own life. Bill Gates' vision wasn't 'a personal computer on my desk' and 'eradicate polio for one person'; it was vast, global and long term.

Selling is service to others: giving the vendor what they want under 'fair exchange'. Earning money is service to others: being remunerated a share of the overall economy of the transaction, under fair exchange. Hiring people to work for you is service to others: supporting their income, helping pay their overheads and contributing to taxes, under fair exchange. Buying material items is service to others: creating jobs and an outlet of passion and creativity of the creator/vendor, under fair exchange. All acts of service create a greater economy and outlet for others to serve in turn. Acts of service aren't one-way; it's not just the seller that serves the vendor, the employee that serves the employer and the parent who serves the child; it is an interconnected web of 360-degree, four-dimensional service that adds or detracts from the economy, progress and, ultimately, evolution.

If a footballer serves his team best by scoring goals, stopping goals or setting up goals, he will be remunerated accordingly. He doesn't just randomly get paid £250,000 a week. His salary and ultimately sponsorship deals and image rights are directly in proportion to the service he provides for his team, his manager and the fans. No footballer will ever get that level of salary if he doesn't pass, save, score or set up any goals. His level of service to his team directly affects the success of his team, and feeds back to his salary. He gets a higher salary than those who add less value and service than him, and a lower salary than those who add more value and service. If he gives no service, he loses his place in the team and ultimately loses his contract. If he increases his service, other teams want to buy him, and will pay high fees and a higher salary.

It irks me when people moan about footballers' salaries. Whether or not you feel that they make their living diving and rolling around and hounding the referee is beside the point. Footballers earn exactly what they are worth in relation to serving others. The best footballers earn the most. The best footballers entertain the most people, giving the most people passion and purpose and hope and enjoyment. The best footballers inspire the most people to want to play football and be as good as them one day. It is the way.

And if it is transient or not deserved, then it corrects itself. If a footballer keeps getting injured, then the owners of the club negotiate a 'pay per play' contract. If the player doesn't live up to the hype or play as well as they did in the previous club, they get sold and their value goes down, as does their salary. If they don't maintain a level of performance or play for the team, they get dropped and sometimes get forced to play with the reserves.

Footballers' salaries are a micro-insight into how the world works regarding serving, solving and remuneration. As footballers get better, they get peripheral deals that earn them more money, sponsorship, endorsements, even paid social-media posts. They have attracted this because of their level of mastery, linked to how it serves and solves for others. This compounds upwards. According to www.thesportbible.com, Cristiano Ronaldo can get paid up to €230,366 per tweet. This is the compounded manifestation of the years of hard work, mastery and level and scale of service to others. And as soon as this value erodes, so does the level of remuneration. Think what happened to Tiger Woods and Lance Armstrong: once things began to unravel, sponsors cancelled their contracts, the media started making demands, and the number of people they served decreased as people changed their perception of them and the value they added to their lives.

Serving and solving are two of the little-known secrets of how to increase our own value, self-worth and remuneration. They are connected and part of the greater whole of our entire species, and the interconnected nature of all species. Even a whole species becomes extinct once it serves no value.

Serving and solving explain accurately why wealth isn't evenly distributed. As ideological as socialism and communism are, they don't encourage serving and solving, which is why capitalism is more prevalent in world social structures and systems. Capitalism balances human self-interest (needed to survive and thrive) with the interconnected personal-and-greater-whole benefit of serving and solving. Socialism and communism discourage self-interest and, if serving and solving and the scale of serving and solving serve the self too, then serving and solving are also discouraged.

You are remunerated in equal balance to the number of people you serve, the scale of the service you provide, the number of problems you solve, and the scale of those problems.

SOME EXAMPLES

Here are some examples of people and companies serving and solving in different areas and at different levels:

- Hans Rausing, son of Tetra Pak® founder Ruben Rausing, has a net worth in excess of £7 billion, partly as a result of the company's most famous innovation: the plastic-covered paper milk carton.

- The Post-it® note: it is estimated that 50 billion Post-it notes are sold each year, generating approximately $1 billion in annual revenue for 3M. The Post-it note was 'invented' by accident in 1968.

- Ken Modestou receives £16,000 for cutting the hair of the Sultan of Brunei, when expenses to travel from the Dorchester Hotel to South-East Asia are added in. Most celebrity hairdressers charge £280 to £1,100 per cut.

- Tetris® the simple computer puzzle game, has sold over 100 million copies.

- *Eclipse*, Roman Abramovich's yacht, is reputed to have cost between $400 million and $ 800 million to build. It has 70 crew, room for 24 guests, two helipads and a submarine.

- Bill Foege has reputedly helped save 131 million lives with his successful global strategy for eradicating smallpox. He now advises the Bill & Melinda Gates Foundation, with a view to eradicating polio. He was awarded the Presidential Medal of Honor in 2012.

Each of these examples above serve and solve in different ways. Here are the ways they serve and solve, and how you can too:

1. Solve a small problem for many people.
2. Solve a big problem for a few people.
3. Solve a small problem multiple times.

4. Solve a big problem multiple times.

5. Serve charitably.

6. Serve materially.

7. Serve by entertainment.

The Post-it® note solves a small, simple problem for many people, many times over, as do the many patents that Tetra Pak® hold. Roman Abramovich's yacht served one person, once, with a huge transactional remuneration, and served materially. Bill Foege served charitably, and would be able to monetize his service and recognition. Tetris® served and solved by entertainment. Ken Modestou served materially (you could say with a vanity service).

The Life Leverage philosophy understands that, if you help enough people get what they want, you will get what you want. Your value is not as a silo but as an interconnected solver of problems and servant to more people, or bigger problems. Your remuneration, IGV (Income-Generating Value) and self-worth are directly linked to your attitude towards and commitment to serving and solving.

> *'If life gets hard for you, help more people and life will help you.'*
> – Rob Moore

> *'The best way to find yourself is to lose yourself in the service of others.'*
> – Mahatma Gandhi

The more money you make for other people, the more money you make for yourself. Increase your focus and scale of serving and solving.

Instead of shying away from big problems, attack them and solve them and your value will increase. As your IGV increases, so does your self-worth and you naturally move to a higher level of remuneration, service and scale. This translates to manifesting your vision and legacy.

Summary

If you want wealth, serve more people. If you want happiness, help more people. Figure out how to turn your passion into your profession and your vocation into your vacation, and serve and solve more through your passion. You can monetize your passion by serving and solving. Growth and progress come from taking on bigger challenges and solving bigger problems for more people.

#13 (Life) Leverage strategies

There are eight main areas or concepts of life that encapsulate what you can 'leverage' using the Life Leverage philosophy:

- Time (life)

- Knowledge

- People/skills

- Money

- Ideas and information

- Work/business

- Home life and family

- Social life and hobbies.

Let's look at each one in more detail.

TIME (LIFE)

As discussed in Chapter 1, 'There's no such thing as "time management"', there's no such thing as 'time management'. It might be worth going over that chapter again. Your aim should be to 'gain' time by 'preserving' time. Because time is a countdown clock that starts the day you are born, and counts down slowly as you live, the more you invest and the less you waste, the more you preserve and the less you spend, the more time you will have to do what you love, with whom you love, when you love.

How you perceive time will directly dictate your ability to control and leverage it. Do you see time as the single most precious commodity to preserve at all costs? Do you see time as a gift and aim to maximize every moment you are graced with? Do you look to multiply and leverage time, or do you get stuck duplicating it? Do you savour and enjoy every moment, living in the present with gratitude, or do you constantly look back to the past with regret and guilt, and to the future with fear and envy?

The time-preserving models and techniques I recommend are described in Section 3 on tactics. As we are all looking for systems and models to get more done in less time, outsource everything and create our ideal mobile lifestyle, you will get many technical epiphanies in *Life Leverage*.

Mini summary

Your aim should be to 'gain' time by 'preserving' time. The more you invest and the less you waste, the more you preserve and the less you spend, the more time you will have to do what you love, with whom you love, when you love.

KNOWLEDGE

If you google 'Warren Buffett tips', the first web page that comes up (at the time of writing) is an article from *Time* magazine and the very top piece of advice is the following:

'Invest in as much of yourself as you can,
you are your own biggest asset by far.'

These wise words are from one of the world's richest man. It would have been reasonable to think that he might have given advice on investing in the stock market, or offered a nugget on value or long-term investing, but the reality is that one of the richest men in the world sees your investment in yourself as your most valuable asset.

According to Will Smith, who has become a huge success in music and film, 'the keys to success are running and reading'. On reading, Will Smith says:

'There have been gazillions of people that have lived before all of us. There's no new problem you could have with your parents, with school, with a bully. There's no new problem that someone hasn't already had and written about in a book.'

Of course, Will Smith doesn't mean read Jilly Cooper and *50 Shades of Grey*; he means non-fiction, self-development, educational 'how to' books, like *Life Leverage*.

According to research done by Tom Corley, the author of *Rich Habits: The daily success habits of wealthy individuals*:

- 11 per cent of rich people read for entertainment, compared to 9 per cent of poor people.

- 85 per cent of rich people read two or more educational, career-related or self-improvement books per month, compared to 15 per cent of poor people.

- 94 per cent of rich people read news publications, including news-papers and blogs, compared to 11 per cent of poor people.

In his extensive research, Corley defines 'rich' as earning $160,000 or more in annual salary and a minimum $3.2 million net worth, and poor as earning a maximum $35,000 annual salary and a net worth of $5,000 or less. He says:

'The rich are voracious readers on how to improve themselves. They're reading self-improvement books, biographies, books about successful people, things like that.'

It's crazy to think how much people spend on cars that depreciate, and on holidays that avoid the pain for a week but compound it when the credit-card bill arrives a month later.

It's crazy to think how much people spend on electronic gadgets that lose 90 per cent of their value in three years or less and on legal (or illegal) substances that have no residual value and cause addictions that cost them hundreds of pounds a month or more – while not spending anything on their 'self-investment', which is anything that increases your knowledge, reduces your risk and increases your 'value' in that area.

Here are the ways you can invest in yourself:

- Read books and listen to audio programmes.

- Attend courses, workshops and seminars.

- Use coaches and mentors.

- Network and mastermind with smart people.

- Watch biographies and documentaries.

- Read intelligent factual publications.

- Subscribe to experts' blogs/websites/social media.

- Question convention and listen intently.

If you make money, you can just as easily lose it, but once you have learned something of value, you can't unlearn it. Applied knowledge is power. Those who know the most or are the best in any niche get remunerated proportionately.

The average boxer's salary, according to the US Bureau of Labor Statistics, is $75,760. The tenth highest-earning boxer of all time, Miguel Cotto, earned $8 million for a single fight. That's 106 times more for one fight than the average yearly salary of the average boxer. The highest-earning boxer of all time for a single fight, Oscar de la Hoya, earned $56 million for that fight – seven times more than the tenth highest-earning fight. Everything is not equal.

If you argue that this is 'skill' or 'talent' rather than knowledge (although skill is 'applied knowledge'), then look at lawyers' salaries. Lawyers earned an average annual salary of $131,990 in 2013, yet the tenth highest-earning lawyer, Ana Quincoces, has a net worth of $8 million. The highest-earning lawyer in the world, according to www.therichest.com, has a net worth of $1.7 billion – 212.5 times the tenth highest-earning lawyer. It is likely that the highest-earning lawyer has more knowledge than the tenth highest-earning lawyer, but nowhere near ten times as much. In fact, if you look at darts scoring averages, you can see that the difference between the best and the rest is very small. Even the difference between the best and the tenth best is relatively small.

Here are the stats for the top ten highest-scoring averages for a televised darts match in 2015:

1. 121.86 Michael van Gerwen, Championship League Darts (CLD) 2012

2. 120.86 Phil Taylor, CLD 2011

3. 120.24 Phil Taylor, CLD 2012

4. 118.66 Phil Taylor, UK Open 2010

5. 118.21 Michael van Gerwen, Perth Masters 2014

6. 118.14 Phil Taylor, European Darts Council (EDC) 2009

7. 117.94 Michael van Gerwen, German Darts Championship 2015

8. 117.35 Phil Taylor, Premier League (PL) 2012

9. 116.90 Michael van Gerwen, PL 2015

10. 116.10 Phil Taylor, PL 2012

You can also see that the world's best ever darts player, Phil Taylor, appears in the list six times and 2015 world number one, Michael van Gerwen, appears four times.

In the Industrial Age people added and created value mostly through manual labour. This mass method of work and value exchange was very limiting to the worker, where their ability to serve, solve and scale was capped, and a humble retirement came only after decades of hard graft and sacrifice, not to mention a lack of control and security.

Today things have evolved. Many of the jobs that manual labourers used to do are now done by machines, drones and automated systems. The factory line is mechanized. The value of manual labour has significantly decreased and the value of 'knowledge workers' has significantly increased. Knowledge workers are workers whose main capital (applied earning capacity) is knowledge. Knowledge workers are sometimes called 'gold collars' because of their high salaries as well as because of their relative independence in controlling the process of their own work; they have more money and more freedom than labourers. So it is certainly true to say that the more you learn the more you earn, when that knowledge is applied.

Let's apply the Life Leverage philosophy to this methodology.

If you invest time and learning to get to the very top of your profession, you are likely to earn a disproportionate, inordinate amount of money, control and freedom. You can leverage this process further by choosing a profession that has a disproportionate, inordinate amount of money, control and freedom compared to other professions or vocations.

When Gemma, the love of my life, became pregnant with our first child, Bobby Moore, I considered at length how I should best bring him up to be a great person. As a first-time father I had no experience, and so I sought out some of the best fathers I knew and the best educators in parenting. People say you can't learn to be a parent, that you can only learn on the job and nothing prepares you. I think that is nonsense. While you will have your own personal experience, and you may have a naive perception of what the reality may be (I certainly did) and that it isn't easy, there are many people who have done a great job of raising great kids, and many people who have studied children's behaviour at length, from whom you can learn, all while having your own unique relationship.

Who do I want my son to be? What values do I want to encourage and instil? What do I want to teach him and what profession do I want to encourage him to follow? Are they all 'equal'? Should I just let him choose and take his own path or encourage and guide him down paths I believe are best and right for him? This is where golf comes in.

According to sporteology.com, golf is the fourth highest-paying profession in the world, behind Formula 1, boxing and baseball. This is based on a like-for-like time frame, but doesn't show the whole story. Taking those top four highest-paying professions, the longest careers in each are:

- Formula 1: Rubens Barrichello – 326 races (18 years measured by number of races, not time frame)

- Boxing: Roberto Duran, 33 years (he got KO'd four times!)

- Baseball: Cap Anson and Nolan Ryan, 27 years

- Golf: Gary Player, 56 years.

Gary Player's career as a professional golfer was almost twice as long as that of any other record sportsman. He never got knocked out, never risked his life, and had a very low chance of injury. He, like many other professional golfers, also had many more options when his career came to an end: the Senior's PGA Tour, commentary/media, equipment endorsement or design, and course design – all of which have continued to pay him handsomely well into his eighties.

So I see golf as a potential career for my son, following the Life Leverage philosophy. He'd also have a mobile life, be able to outsource virtually all work that didn't involve hitting golf balls, and merge his passion and profession. At three years old, he was the youngest ever person to get a hole in one (unofficially, as it was not recorded on video – but as if I was going to say to him 'Wait, Bobby, I just need to get my iPhone out as you are going to get a hole in one this next shot and I must get it on video for the Guinness World Record to be valid'), he won his first official golf competition at four years old, beating 11- and 12-year-olds by five and six shots in a six-hole competition, and will be playing in the under-sevens world championships at five years old.

While he is hitting the balls and I am vicariously experiencing the golf career I wanted through him, I feel the Life Leverage philosophy of planning and applied knowledge has helped us get to this point. There are no guarantees in life and this space is to be watched, but I am convinced Bobby Moore will be the world's number-one golfer and win a major before he is 25. If he does, Ladbrokes will be writing me a nice cheque.

> *'You are your best asset, you pay yourself*
> *the best interest, invest in yourself wisely.'*
> *– Rob Moore*

Mini summary

The best way to reduce risk is to leverage knowledge. The more you learn, the more you earn. Invest in yourself wisely. Growth and progress come from knowledge, and all the information you need to become who you want to become is out there; you just need to learn it.

PEOPLE/SKILLS

People/skills means leveraging the skills of other people. When you went to school, you had teachers, who understood their subjects better than you. Your parents paid a lot of money to put you through school, even if your school wasn't private, and it is a societal norm that it's OK to leave your children for a greater percentage of their waking day in the good hands of teachers.

When you took your driving lessons, you used a qualified instructor. When you got your 30-metre badge that you proudly stitched on to your swimwear, you had learned from someone who could swim well. When you go to the doctor you put trust and faith into the white coats and prescriptions. You trust that you'll get the correct diagnosis and dosage of a drug that could kill you if taken in excess.

So, why is it that most people don't have the same faith, attitude and behaviour in business and life? Why do most people mock 'self-help'? Why don't people have coaches, trainers and mentors to help create their ideal life? Why don't people get relationship advice, business coaches and money mentors?

In many of the most important things in life, people are usually feeling their way in the dark, having to make all the mistakes themselves without guidance, support or accountability. By contrast, the rich and successful invest continually and heavily in coaches, mentors and their network.

If you were to Google 'Bill Gates tips', the first page that comes up (at the time of writing) has Bill Gates' famous ten tips on business and becoming rich. The second one is 'Enter in(to) partnerships'.

Here's the extended quote:

'Bill Gates was very fond of forming partnerships with people, people who were the Top Dog and that made Gates become the "Sidekick". He was happy with this, because it unlocked new opportunities for him and the potential to learn from other successful entrepreneurs who could teach him a thing or two.'

Bill Gates has frequently been listed as the richest person in the world. The Harvard dropout credits part of his success to his mentor, businessman and investor Warren Buffett. During an interview with CBC, Gates credited Buffett for teaching him how to deal with tough situations and how to think long-term. Gates also greatly admires Buffett's 'desire to teach things that are complex and put them in a simple form, so that people can understand and get the benefit of all his experience'.

The 'chain of mentors' doesn't stop at the top; it's why and how they get to the top. After Buffett read Benjamin Graham's book *The Intelligent Investor*, the author became his idol. As Buffett has shared in a video clip, the book changed not only his investment philosophy but also the course of his life. Buffett applied to Columbia Business School where Graham was a professor. There, Buffett got to know his idol personally. Later, Graham hired Buffett to work at his company, and the two cemented a strong friendship that led to and had a big impact on Buffett's transformation into the billionaire investor he is today.

Like Buffett, George Soros, one of the most successful contrarian investors of all time, sought out his mentor by a similar means. This billionaire investor is an ardent believer in the principle of fallibilism, the philosophical notion that anything one believes may, in fact, be wrong and therefore worth questioning. A belief in fallibilism has helped Soros consistently challenge and stay ahead of prevailing market wisdom. Fallibilism suggests that you can't continue to grow and learn without outside help, because you can't question something in a different way from the way you question it, only someone outside can. Someone outside, with vast experience in that field or a transmutable one is a greater part of what a mentor is.

These ideas of fallibilism owe much to the philosopher and former London School of Economics professor Karl Popper, a mentor whom Soros intentionally sought out. As Soros revealed, he chose to study under Popper after his book *The Open Society and Its Enemies* 'made a deep impression'.

In an interview with American talk-show host Charlie Rose, Mark Zuckerberg talked about his inspiring mentor, Steve Jobs. 'He was amazing,' said Zuckerberg. 'I had a lot of questions for him.' He described how Jobs gave him advice about how he could build a team that was as focused as Zuckerberg on building 'high quality and good things'.

The usually unflappable Simon Cowell, the producer of the highly successful TV shows *X-Factor* and *American Idol,* has discussed turning to a mentor, billionaire British businessman Sir Phillip Green, after feeling overwhelmed by life. In a candid interview with *The Guardian,* Cowell disclosed that he had experienced difficulty in coping. 'I was trying to deal with everything – my business, the artists, the shows, everything.'

'He's incredibly well-meaning,' Cowell said of Green. 'And very kind. He became someone I could always go to. He makes you confront everything and find a solution.'

'If you ask any successful businessperson, they will always (say they) have had a great mentor at some point along the road.'
– Richard Branson

Branson wrote in a British newspaper: 'It's always good to have a helping hand at the start. I wouldn't have got anywhere in the airline industry without the mentorship of Sir Freddie Laker.'

Branson believes the first step to finding a great mentor is admitting you can benefit from a mentor. 'Understandably there's a lot of ego, nervous energy and parental pride involved, especially with one or two person start-ups. Going it alone is an admirable, but foolhardy and highly flawed approach to taking on the world.'

This is a profound and important statement. Common sense and evidence (as we have seen in this chapter) make it a simple logistical, intelligent decision to have mentors, coaches and an extended network of skilled people. So why don't most people invest in these important areas? Why do they see it as a cost rather than an investment? Why don't they prioritize this?

Let's look at each of the reasons separately:

1. Lack of knowledge

2. The expense

3. Fear

4. Envy

5. Delusion.

1. Lack of knowledge

They don't know what they don't know. They don't know what a mentor really is, or just how much they can help. This section should, I hope, have given the knowledge and proven the value of a mentor.

2. The expense

'Mentors cost too much to hire. I can't afford it. I'm not sure it will pay a return on investment.' The thing is, free advice is worth every penny. You get what you pay for, so, when finding a mentor, make sure that they are the real deal in the area you are looking to learn about, and if they are cheap, be very sceptical. You want to find and hire the best, if you want the best. If many of the richest and most successful people living on the planet attribute much of their success to having mentors, then it goes without saying that the same result will work for you. See it as an investment, not a cost, and move money from depreciating liabilities and start investing it in yourself.

3. Fear

'It might not work. It might cost money. I might not be good enough.' This sounds as though you really do need a mentor. The worst that is likely to happen is that it doesn't quite work out, you learn and grow from the experience, and you move on. The best that could happen is unfathomably high. Rich list? Best in the world? Who knows?

4. Envy

This is conscious or unconscious jealousy of someone else's success, perhaps a feeling that it was easier for them, they had a better upbringing, more money, inherited it all. Your ego battles hard to defend its position, and anyone who appears to be successful challenges your very being.

Seeing someone else as a success can point out harsh truths about one's own life that the ego doesn't want to admit or wants to excuse or blame. This can be the hardest/biggest barrier to success, and serves only to block progress and growth towards your vision.

5. Delusion

'I don't need help. I can do it on my own. No one can tell me how to run my [life, business; whatever].' Since you make mistakes and learn from them, on the job, this is a delusion of the highest order.

Having coaches, trainers and mentors should be one of your highest-priority KRAs. Building your extended network of experts with decades of experience is the Life Leverage way of genuinely and sustainably shortcutting the time and effort to achieve your vision.

Leveraging their time, expertise and thousands of hours served gives you results as close as possible to theirs, in a fraction of the time. Mentors and coaches preserve your time, and maximize getting more done in less time.

For more detail on the 'how to', see the next chapter, 'Network and mastermind (Life) Leverage'.

Mini summary

Leveraging the knowledge and skills of other people, particularly those more experienced than you in the field you are in, is, without a doubt, one of the best ways to improve your skills quickly and efficiently, leading you on the road to success faster than if you were to learn by trial and error on your own. All the greats had mentors. Learn from the best if you want to be the best.

MONEY

You can work hard for your money, or your money can work hard for you. You can be a slave to money, or money can be a servant to you. You can exchange time for money, or you can build assets that create passive income that preserves your time.

There are fundamental differences in beliefs, attitudes, strategies and behaviours around money between the 'poor' and the 'rich', the 'business owner' and the 'employee'.

Here are the main 'poor' money beliefs:

- You have to work hard to make money.

- Earning money is hard.

- Money doesn't grow on trees.

- Money is the root of all evil.

- Money doesn't buy happiness / make you happy.

- Capitalism / making money is greedy.

- I have to pay all my bills and expenses first.

- My friends won't like me / will judge me if I make money / change.

These beliefs are very real to the beholder, but in fact they are a projected, deluded reality of an individual person that is true for them but only them. Every human being has their own individual and unique values and beliefs, based on their own individual and unique life experiences, friends and family (especially parents or primary carers), geographic location, schooling, religion or higher belief, media exposure, and so on.

We convince ourselves that what we see is the single and only one reality, when it is only our reality as a unique individual. Therefore all reality is delusion, because it isn't reality, just reality to us. This 'reality' is firm and we hold on to it, especially and particularly around money. But if one person on the planet can have money and a good healthy relationship with money, so can you.

If we are, therefore, all delusionally connected to one individual reality that isn't the single reality, then surely it makes sense to become conscious of that reality (values, beliefs, attitudes), and make it serve and empower us to reach our vision and live out our highest values. And, like it or not, it is most likely that a lack of money will slow that vision down, and an abundance of money will speed it up significantly.

Here are the main poor money beliefs again, and how the wealthy have an opposing belief to counter them.

- **You have to work hard to make money.**

You have to make money work hard for you by investing in assets that create passive income.

- **Earning money is hard.**

Making and creating money is a relatively easy system and process that is learnable like anything else; you just have to focus on it.

- **Money doesn't grow on trees.**

Yes it does, it's made of paper. Money is abundant and everywhere, in almost limitless supply.

- **Money is the root of all evil.**

Money is the cause of all good. Money cures disease. Money creates charity. Money buys time to give back. Money solves problems.

- **Money doesn't buy happiness / make you happy.**

Actually, it does!

- **Capitalism / making money is greedy.**

Capitalism is what allows any individual to make a fair living, merging self-interest and service in equal balance. Making money creates economy, service, employment, taxes and benefits to others.

- **I have to pay all my bills and expenses first.**

I pay myself first, and bills and overheads later/after.

- **My friends won't like me / will judge me if I make money / change.**

Change is healthy, natural and, if you don't grow, you die. I can/will become a better person with more wealth. If my friends really are friends they will grow with me, and if they aren't it's OK to let them go.

Only once values, beliefs and attitudes around money are changed to serve your vision, and become empowering rather than restricting, can money start to flow your way. I could write an entire book on this subject; in fact, it will be my next/eighth book. Let's move on, assuming you have embraced these more serving, empowering beliefs and attitudes towards money, and you see it as a vehicle to serve and solve and to help achieve your vision.

MONEY – THE LIFE LEVERAGE WAY

The Life Leverage way of making money is through maximum income generation/creation, with minimum time exchange, under fair exchange. The *only* way to create income and capital, and still preserve time, is through assets. You invest time and capital (where relevant/necessary) in assets that produce (passive) income, you set them up, get them managed by people or systems, then you exclude yourself from the operation of them.

The types of asset you can build, which will each be detailed in Section 4, on the Mobile Lifestyle Blueprint, are as follows:

- a business (physical, e-commerce)

- property

- intellectual property (ideas/patents/licences/information/music)

- investments (stocks, bonds, paper, etc.)

- moneylending

- physical assets (precious metals, art, watches, wine, classic cars)

- partnerships (franchise, joint ventures, etc.).

If you don't have any of these working for you, you will be working for your money. You will be spending your time rather than investing, leveraging and preserving it.

There are six levels of using money. They can form a wealth hierarchy, if ordered and leveraged correctly, and in the right order:

Level 1. Spending (want, need)

Level 2. Saving

Level 3. Investing

Level 4. Speculating

Level 5. Insuring

Level 6. Giving.

Let's explore these.

Level 1. Spending (need, want)

Spending on necessities comes first: spending on basic survival. But most people can actually live on a lot less than they think or have become accustomed and addicted to – making 'want' spending 'need' spending. You need less than you think you need.

Want spending is what keeps most people poor. They spend money on liabilities or perishables that decay in value quickly and produce no capital or income residual.

According to the investment company Scottish Widows, 9 million people (one in five) in the UK have no savings at all. That is around 15 per cent of the population. Of those, 20 per cent rely on their monthly wages to cope. According to a More study, 33 per cent of UK residents have less than £500 in savings to their name. Only 12 per cent of UK residents have £50,000 or more in savings/investments (only two years' humble living expenses for a couple). The average person in the UK has £343 in disposable income and £4,300 in savings; 21 per cent of Americans don't even have a savings account and 62 per cent of Americans have less than $1,000 dollars in savings.

The biggest difference between the rich and poor is that the rich 'spend' (invest) money on assets that produce (passive) income. They then spend income that is residual and gets replaced by the asset, on liabilities and perishables. They preserve the time and capital, and money that recurs is used for spending, allowing the capital to grow.

Level 2. Saving

The first stage of mastering money management is saving. It sounds obvious. Results prove it isn't. Saving is the discipline of holding money for the long term rather than spending it in the short term. Saving is the foundation of wealth. Saving is the roots that bear the fruits. It teaches fundamentals that build wealth, such as delaying gratification, discipline and basic money management.

But, despite the power of compounding, saving alone will not create vast wealth, service and your life's vision. The problem with saving alone is that it rear-loads all the benefits. It does not follow the Life Leverage philosophy. Here's an example of the power but also the limitation of saving alone, and not moving on to Levels 3 to 6.

A live scenario posted on one of my online communities was a question from Matthew Watson: *'Rob, if I want to save £300 per month, that's £3,600 a year, the interest is low, so how will the law of compounding make much difference?'*

Here is my answer: 'Matthew, yes it's only £3,600 a year. Let's assume you could beat inflation by a net 2 per cent. End of year 1 – £3,672, end of year 2 – £7,414.44 (interest worked out earned on full 12 months), end of year 3 – £11,237.78, end of year 4 – £15,135.54, end of year 5 – £19,109.23 …

- End of year 10 – £40,207.37

- End of year 15 – £63,501.42

- End of year 25 – £120,842.01

- End of year 35 – £187,513.12

- End of year 50 – £325,858.77

'It took 15 years to get to £63,501, but the last 15 years gave over £138,000. If you make it just 3 per cent net, here are the figures:

- Year 1 – £3,782.16

- Year 3 – £11,690.27

- Year 5 – £20,080

- Year 10 – £43,358.22

- Year 25 – £137,894.71

- Year 50 – £438,585.50.'

So, you see a dichotomy. On the one hand, you can see how compounding builds momentum, and the longer you give it to grow, the more powerful it is. You can also see that small amounts at the start will return more and make a bigger difference at the end.

But it takes years and years to build its power. Even at year 50, saving £300 per calendar month and getting a 3 per cent net return on it gives only £438,585.50. At 5 per cent net, yearly passive income from that capital sum, after 50 years of saving, gives you £21,929 a year to live on. But in 50 years that would have been eroded by inflation and, as such, would not hold as much value. The average price of property in the UK 50 years ago was £3,465, according to house price data provided by Nationwide. That buys an average second-hand car now. So what will a small yearly salary 'buy' in 50 years' time? Maybe a week's food shopping?

So, while saving is a vital part of the growth and journey towards more money and Life Leverage wealth, it is not enough.

Level 3. Investing

Saving comes before investing, because investing has more risks. If you lose your investment (which can happen) and have no savings supporting it, you lose everything. Once you have a foundational savings pot, for, say, six to 12 months' living expenses, then you can start using some of the money you were putting away as savings, to invest.

When you start investing, you should look for relatively low-risk investments with a relatively low knowledge barrier. Stocks, property and a business venture you have knowledge in are probably the lowest barriers from a standing start, as the risks are low (if invested properly) compared to more volatile or speculative alternatives.

In an economic sense, an investment is the purchase of goods that are not consumed today but are used in the future to create wealth. In finance, an investment is a monetary asset purchased with the idea that the asset will provide income in the future or appreciate and be sold at a higher price.

Level 4. Speculating

Many people speculate with the idea that they are investing. Speculation is higher-risk investing, with greater potential for reward. If you speculate before you invest (say, invest in a start-up business you know little about), you risk losing both your investment and your savings. You should move up to speculation only once you've gained investment knowledge and skill, your investments de-risk and protect potential speculative loss, and you need to diversify your investment.

Speculation may be investing in something you have little or no knowledge about, be more volatile or cyclical, have less proven data for success (tech investments), be very niche with technical knowledge required (watches, wine, art), or simply something that was a gamble that you convinced yourself was an investment.

Level 5. Insuring

This is a nice problem. Once you have wealth, the world tries to take some of it from you, to teach you to grow. Once you get to a certain level of wealth, you need to insure against loss or attack as much as you need to make more. You explore insurance through diversification, tax reduction and protection.

As your wealth increases, so do your tax levels. As you gain more material items, maintenance costs go up and your risk of theft or damage goes up. As you have more money, more people and charities want you to give it away to them.

You insure your wealth by diversifying your investments and insuring against risk, theft, loss and investigations. Instead of flaunting it, you hide it. Protection becomes more important than creation.

Level 6. Giving

Once you have moved up through the five levels, you can then give back. Of course, you can continually give back via donating a percentage of your income or, better, donating your time and experience into something where you can make a real difference and that means something to you. Wealth through the five levels buys/frees time to do this.

Poor people with poor money beliefs often give too much away too early because they have guilt, fear and shame around money. Others never give any away and are self-centred, but society finds a way of gaining balance back.

The further up the levels you go, the more your knowledge becomes more valuable than your money, to make money. You gain insights and experience into 'no money down' investing, people investing their money into you, and joint-venture partnerships where people invest to buy your time and experience.

Mini summary

Many people have a false perception of money. There are 'poor' beliefs, such as 'Money doesn't grow on trees' or 'Money is the root of all evil', often instilled into us by others as we are growing up. We convince ourselves that these are facts and that money will not make us happy. But that just isn't true. Money is also the cause of all good. Money can help to solve problems. And money can make you happy ... if you know what to do with it and how to use it properly. There are six levels of using money. You have to move up the ranks, knowing how to spend, save, invest, speculate, insure and, finally, give. The more knowledge you acquire at each level, the more money you will make.

IDEAS AND INFORMATION

A major innovation of the twenty-first century is how information has become a kind of currency. The value of information has increased, and what was intangible, and therefore hard to value, has become a strong mechanism for exchange, monetization and leverage. This has accelerated through three recent 'ages' – from the Industrial Age to the Information Age, and the Information Age to the current Technology Age.

Before the Information Age was the Industrial Age, a period of history encompassing changes in economic and social organization that began around 1760 in Great Britain, and later in other countries, characterized chiefly by the replacement of hand tools with power-driven machines such as the power loom and the steam engine, and by the concentration of industry in large establishments.

In the Industrial Age, machines replaced many manual labour roles. Those who embraced working with machines, owning and running factory lines, such as Henry Ford, became the world's most powerful and wealthiest people. Those who didn't learn how to work with and leverage machinery and automation got left behind; their value and earning capacity diminished.

Before the Technology Age was the Information Age, a period beginning around 1975 and characterized by the gathering and almost instantaneous transmission of vast amounts of information and by the rise of information-based industries.

The Information Age was – and to some extent continues to be – a time when large amounts of information were widely available to many people, largely through computer technology, characterized by the shift from traditional industry to an economy based on information computerization.

The onset of the Information Age is associated with the Digital Revolution, just as the Industrial Revolution marked the onset of the Industrial Age. As in the Industrial Age, workers who perform tasks that are easily automated have been forced to find work that involves tasks that are not easily automated, of which there are fewer and fewer as technology multiplies. Workers, who were replaced by machines in the Industrial Age, are being replaced by computers and technology in the Information and Technology Ages.

The Information Age has affected the workforce, in that automation and computerization have resulted in higher productivity coupled with net job loss. In the United States, for example, from January 1972 to August 2013, the number of people employed in manufacturing jobs fell from 17,500,000 to 11,500,000, while manufacturing value rose 270 per cent. This is being even more extremely compounded by the Technology Age we are in today when it is easier than ever to start and scale a start-up company thanks to the technology that disrupts and attacks the big corporations.

Workers are also being forced to compete in a global job market, so competition for jobs has significantly increased. Jobs traditionally associated with the working class (assembly-line workers, data processors, foremen and supervisors) have dramatically reduced in volume as they have become increasingly unnecesary either through outsourcing or automation through both the Information and Technology Ages.

Individuals who lost their jobs in the Information Age had two choices: move up, joining a group of 'knowledge workers' (engineers, doctors, attorneys, teachers, scientists, professors, executives, journalists, consultants), or settle for low-skill, low-wage service jobs. Most people fell into the latter group. Individuals who lost their jobs in the Technology Age also had polarized choices: disrupt and start your own enterprise, leverage, outsource and scale through technology, or once again settle for a high-skilled but lower-paying role or even a lower-skilled service-based job.

To think that two 'ages' have occurred since 1975, in a period of only four decades or so, is quite amazing. By contrast, the Industrial Age started 215 years before the Information Age.

Change is accelerating and so is the attrition of change. The upside is huge for those who embrace change, but the fallout and ease of getting left behind are far greater, and more compounded too.

INFORMATION MARKETING

The single biggest feature of the Information Age and its increase in value is the speed at which it moves, and therefore the speed at which you can access, consume and share it. Humans have got better at leveraging the speed of information. Centuries ago information moved at the speed a horse could be ridden. Globally, it could move as fast as a ship. Then, locally, it could move as fast as a train could travel, then, even more locally, as fast as a car could be driven, then globally as fast a plane could fly. In between, information could travel as fast as Morse code or radio waves. Then planes got faster and information could travel faster than the speed of sound at 343.2 metres per second.

Today information can travel at the speed of a microwave, and at the speed of light through fibre optics, at almost 300,000 kilometres per second. This is game changing: information is becoming a currency and even a commodity.

You can learn faster than ever. You can learn from home, or anywhere in the world, from anyone in the world, from all the information in the world. You can self-teach anything, and Google has handily organized most of the world's information for you in a convenient and fast-access filing system to reduce your time and maximize your leverage.

You can instantly access and learn any language, learn an instrument tutored by your favourite musician, learn a sport from your sports heroes and model your style on your favourite celebrity. You can even engage with them through social media. And you can learn and access all this information at the speed of light in multiple convenient formats such as audio, video and text. You can get bite-sized chunks to consume on the go, in the form of blogs, 30-minute audio summaries and/or Twitter and Instagram.

Ideas and information at the speed of light can give you knowledge it took the people before you decades to master. It can increase your value and ability to serve. You can maximize leverage and time preservation, and eradicate time wastage and cost.

Perhaps the most powerful currency of information is information marketing. Selling information has become one of the biggest innovations and growth industries.

Around 98 per cent of all information is now digital. Every minute, at the time of writing, the following happens in the digital world: 204 million emails are sent, 47,000 apps are downloaded, £57,000 in sales are made, 61,141 hours of audio are downloaded, 3,000 photos are uploaded, 20 million photos are viewed, 100,000 new tweets are tweeted, ten new Wikipedia articles are published, 6 million Facebook pages are viewed, 2 million Google searches are made, 30 hours of video are uploaded and 1.3 million videos are viewed.

'Information marketing' – the selling of information – is a modern industry worth more than $100 billion worldwide, growing 32.7 per cent from the previous year.

Four billion people use email, 79 per cent of the population use social media, 61 per cent use e-newsletters, 51 per cent use blogs, 42 per cent use webinars and 16 per cent use podcasts.

Compare this to traditional print media, where only 39 per cent use printed magazines and 25 per cent printed newsletters. Forty-four per cent of direct postal mail is never opened, 86 per cent of people skip TV ads and 54 per cent more leads are generated by information marketing than by traditional marketing. Three-quarters of business decision-makers prefer to get company information in a series of articles rather than via an advertisement.

As manual labourers become less valuable and replaced by systems, machines and technology, information becomes more valuable in the age of the knowledge and technology worker. Information becomes easier to sell because it is the new commodity, due to its speed of movement and the multiple outlets that reach billions of people in fractions of a second. You can sell your ideas. You can sell your knowledge and experience.

You can sell your music. You can even sell your rants and your tweets. You can sell them through free social-media channels that reach billions of people in a fraction of a second. You can set up an online presence or 'shopfront' for next to nothing, exchange money on portals like PayPal, and you have a business as long as you can get a Wi-Fi signal.

Your information business is about as low-risk as a business could be. There is no stockholding, inventory or overhead. You can run your business from home without the need for premises and long leases, and you can do it from anywhere in the world in your free time, with a global customer base.

You can sell the same/similar piece of low-cost information millions of times; there is no 'download stock limit'. You can repackage and repurpose that information and sell it hosted online, in physical book format, on CD, DVD, audiobook, Kindle, iTunes, Audible, iBooks, iTunes U, on a paid membership site platform, in a seminar room, on a mentorship or mastermind programme, or on a retreat.

Information marketing is selling the Life Leverage philosophy. You create and set your product once, as in this book, and you can earn on it many times over. Once the product is created, it can generate residual, passive, recurring income for years or decades to come. It can go viral and get shared and sold by affiliates and resellers and social-media addicts. Information and ideas marketing are quite possibly the most leveraged use of time, giving maximum return with minimum wastage. There is virtually no duplication of time and each medium of information you create is a genuine asset if leveraged effectively.

You have unique talents, skills and expertise. In at least one specific area, you are better than most people on the planet. The pains that people are experiencing in this area you can solve quickly through the above outlets and media.

You can serve and solve many people; you just didn't know you could or didn't know your value. Until now, that is. Almost everyone has a book in them; the thing is for most people it is still in them. Get your information out there. Serve more people with your unique genius, and get paid handsomely (and passively) for it.

Mini summary

With the speed of information increasing all the time, information has now become a kind of currency. You can learn anything you desire, from anyone, anywhere in the world. Whether you want to learn a new skill or increase your knowledge of a topic you are interested in, this new Technology Age, with its free and speed-of-light transfer of information, means that you can have the information at hand almost immediately. Using this to market your talents is key to the Life Leverage philosophy. You can make money passively, and repeatedly, by sharing your knowledge, thoughts and/or ideas in many media or packaged formats through the many online platforms.

WORK/BUSINESS

The Life Leverage philosophy merges passion and profession, vocation and vacation, as much as possible. The more you try to live a dual life of wishing you were at home when you're at work, and dreading going back to work when you're at home, the more disconnected and dissatisfied you will be. Most people work to live, but most of the people who make a difference, change the world or live a fulfilling life are working to live.

At any time in your life, whether just starting your career or nearing retirement age, you could and should ask yourself: 'Is this business or career I'm in what I really want to do?'

If it is, you will endure, even enjoy the challenge and sacrifice because it is a worthy journey and vision for you. Dr David J. Lieberman states that happiness is 'the progress towards a worthy goal'. That progress is sometimes fast, sometimes slow, and sometimes it seems as if it is standing still. But as long as there is clarity of vision, there is always progress towards a worthy goal.

According to care2.com, number one on the list 'Ten things unhappy people have in common' is that they 'hate their jobs'.

According to many sources and studies, your vocation is both the source of much content and much misery, and therefore it is a high-priority, high-KRA function to make sure of five things:

1. You are in the right vocation.

2. You are doing the right things in your vocation.

3. You are merging passion and profession where possible.

4. You have the right people around you in your vocation.

5. You are regularly measuring/evaluating numbers 1 to 4 above.

1. You are in the right vocation.

You know intuitively if you are in the right vocation. If you are, good for you; you're a rare breed. Keep doing your thing and making a difference. I salute you. If you aren't, you need to make a plan or a change right now. Either do what you know you should have done years ago and make the change, or create a specific timelined plan with accountability to the 'end date' and set about replacing your vocation and doing what you need to do to get there. Do *not* make excuses, do *not* let yourself off the hook, do *not* fear the short-term dip in income or hardship or learning a new skill. You are way more resourceful than you are giving yourself credit for, and you get only one life. So *make* it happen. Now.

2. You are doing the right things in your vocation.

If you are in the right vocation, but doing the wrong things, that is not living the Life Leverage philosophy. Follow the VVKIK exercise in this book and get yourself back on track doing the right role that makes the biggest difference to you and your vision, and makes the best use of your time and skills.

Get yourself out of all the admin. Ask to be moved to a different department. Get your KRAs and IGTs rewritten. Do it now.

3. You are merging passion and profession where possible.

Separating home life from work life will make you feel bipolar. You will feel that you should be at home when you are at work, and at work when you are at home, enjoying neither and never experiencing the gift of the present moment. And then you'll be 75 wondering where your life went. There are some strategies in the next chapter that will help merge your vocation and vacation.

4. You have the right people around you in your vocation.

Having the right coaches and mentors around you is vital for your growth. If you are in a career, it is vital that you have great people around you in your company that you respect and can learn from. Make sure that you have a great boss who can teach you, support you and help you progress. Make sure that you are in a team with diverse skills so your non-skills can be outsourced and leveraged. You don't always have to like them, but you do need to respect them for their skills and feel that they can help you progress towards your vision.

5. You are regularly measuring/evaluating numbers 1 to 4 above.

Every August and December, take time for yourself, by yourself or with your family, to evaluate numbers 1 to 4. Just make sure that you're going in the right direction and you haven't veered off course or been pulled away from your vision. If you check in every six months, your changes will be minor tweaks, and you will be only very slightly off course at worst. If you take ten years to do this, your life could be too far gone to have time to get it back. Book the diary entries in your calendar now. Name it 'My vision meeting with myself'. Make it recur indefinitely and write after it 'DO NOT REMOVE'.

Keep learning and you'll keep earning. The more you know, the more you'll grow.

Mini summary

You know whether you are in the right vocation. If you're not, then it's time to make a change. Now. Working towards a worthy goal is easy when you know how. Follow the five simple steps to make sure that your KRAs function at a high level. Choose the right vocation, do the right things, merge your passion with your profession, have the right people around you and regularly evaluate where you are, and you will grow more in the direction you want to, and more quickly. Do it now.

HOME LIFE AND FAMILY

Too much 'work' and you have unrest at home. Too much home time and you can't make enough money, progress your career or make a dent in the universe. Either way, sacrifice causes inner conflict and resentment on at least one side, and sometimes affects both. But why do life and work have to be so separate and compartmentalized?

Don't make sacrifices on either side or strive to achieve balance, as 'balance' is so rarely possible. Like a pendulum that swings from one extreme to the other, things rarely sit for long in the centre. So to think we can be in a constant state of balancing work and life is at best very hard and at worst futile. The Life Leverage way of achieving the 'work–life balance' is to live them both simultaneously, so you don't have to struggle for balance or make sacrifices.

I'm not saying you should be checking your emails while you're holding the baby; I've tried that and you drop either the phone or the baby! I'm saying you can be on holiday with the family, and have business meetings in the morning while your children are at KidZania. I'm saying you could book a public-speaking gig in another country and take your family on a mini-holiday. If your specialized subject can serve them, bring your family and they can learn from you. Put your children in a good school and drum up some business or finance raising from the parents. Take your children to their party and write a chapter of your book (I did this yesterday, got one whole chapter written while Bobby was at the bowling alley, and got invited to dinner by a fellow property investor). Take your family away when you book courses, trainings and conferences, instead of having to be away from them.

Go out for dinner with business owners and wealthy individuals you can learn from. Make some of your nights out a network-building vocation/vacation. Play golf with millionaires. Join the best clubs and gyms for your hobbies and fitness so you can meet great people. View property while you are travelling. Find out if there are seminars in the countries you visit. Meet your family at lunchtime. Live in more than one country; spend the summer months in the UK, the winter months 'living' in Dubai or Tenerife or Florida or Grand Cayman for the duration of the school holidays.

When embarking on a new vocation, people often struggle with balance. If you are in that position now, or you are spinning too many plates, sit down with the important people in your life, and plan and book evergreen time with them, in the diary: holidays, date nights, family time and so on. If something is in the diary and can't be moved, everything else fills time and space around it. If it isn't, then it gets superseded and no space is left. The more in advance these are booked in, the more the world will move all tasks and gigs and trips around these, and you will be able to do both with the least amount of sacrifice.

I hated holidays, and Gemma, the love of my life, hated that I hated holidays. I'd do it begrudgingly every five years, feeling like it was a waste of time and that I wasn't progressing, and would end up working all the time out of choice while she was horizontal on the beach all day. I'd have constant ants in my pants and I think it drove her mad. Now we merge all work-related events (Monaco, Grand Cayman, Florida, Dubai) with family holidays, so, where possible, work and life become one passion, vocation and vacation. Gemma gets to relax and have multiple holidays, we take the children, they are involved in my 'work' life and I am heavily involved in their lives. A bit of work and a bit of play each day and we all get our needs met.

I run public-speaking retreats in Florida and we play golf with my son in the time off. I run mentorship/mastermind programmes in Grand Cayman and the family get to do amazing things. Gemma gets involved in the event management so she has independence and self-worth time away from the children from time to time. We go to the Monaco Grand Prix every year, spend time with amazing people, many of them celebrities, and the family has a great time while our network grows.

You can use the same Life Leverage philosophy to blur the lines of work and play. In merging travel and holiday, work and play, both Gemma and I are able to get our needs and values met. Because everyone on the planet has different values, it's not always easy to keep everyone in your family happy. The absolute must-do with your family is to learn one other's values. Ask your partner and your children, 'What's the most important thing to you in your life?' a few times over, without projecting that it should involve you, and you will have a blueprint of how to love them, serve them, live with them and also how to influence them when you particularly want something that is important to you. You will have access to knowledge most people don't have of those they love, and you can build a life for your family that meets all your needs and values. This is what happened when we merged 'work' trips with holidays; all of our family got their values met.

You want to know the values of the closest people to you. In addition to your family this might mean your business partner, best friends, boss, managing director or main subordinates – anyone important who assists you closely in your vision or is a big part of your life. A true win–win and sustainable relationship is where both parties are having their individual values honoured. Get your family and key partners involved in your business planning, goal setting and vision. Have a family vision meeting every year where each family member contributes to the overall family values and vision. Set goals with your children from a young age so they are able to achieve a worthy aim, feel good and learn skills that will hold them in good stead for life. Again, you can do this on a work–play holiday.

The less you separate the work and life, and the more ways you find to organize and compartmentalize time, merging passion with profession and vocation with vacation, the longer you will stay in the business, the bigger a legacy you will leave, and you'll have a great relationship with your children, and your partner, too.

Mini summary

Make work–life balance a conscious decision to live them both simultaneously instead of sacrificing one for the other. You can merge functions like travel, holidays, shopping, investing, research and vision so they serve your passion and profession together. You can include your friends and family in work, and work in your social life, so that you live one complete, whole life instead of always thinking about work at home and wishing you were home at work.

SOCIAL LIFE AND HOBBIES

In much the same way, you can merge your hobbies and social life with your profession, just as you can your home and family life. Use the Life Leverage philosophy socially, too. If you don't have (m)any hobbies, choose ones where you will meet the right kind of people that could serve and grow your network.

Join the best clubs you can afford. Have meetings at the gym or set up a gym at work and do your calls while on your exercise bike (tell them first or they'll think you're weird). Merge a dinner out with a possible business venture. If you want to go shopping or go to the theatre, go the night before an event or seminar, and merge the two. Go on a course and reward your day with a trip to, say, Harrods. Instead of watching garbage on TV, watch educational and inspirational documentaries on successful people and companies. Instead of reading trashy novels, read self-development books. Use social media for business. Have friends you can learn from.

Mini summary

Reread this section; it was short yet so important. Stop sacrificing and start merging social and business for a more complete life the Life Leverage way.

Summary

Stop sacrificing and start merging social and business for a more complete life the Life Leverage way. You can redefine both. Work doesn't have to be 'work' anymore. You can write the rules of your life. You don't have to delay everything you want to do until your time runs out.

#14 Network and mastermind (Life) Leverage

Most people are working too hard to be rich. Most people think that working harder on more operational tasks is going to lead to an early retirement of doing nothing. They are deluded.

If you study the people perceived by society as having been the most successful, the ones that movies are made about and statues are built of, most of them were visionaries and strategists. And every single one of them, without exception, had one thing in common: they had great people around them. The people could have been in the form of a great wife to a powerful man (or vice versa), great employees for a business owner, great team members for a sportsperson, great mentors, coaches and advisors, great agents, accountants, tax advisors, great sages and muses and spiritual healers.

Your network is your net worth. And your relationship with that network defines the amount of money you leverage from it. One of the biggest factors in your success will come down to your long-term relationships and the trust you build, creating goodwill and leverage from your contact base who will work hard serving you and in harmony with your vision. The more business you generate for your network and the more money you help them make by giving them employment or contracts, the more money you will make.

One of my passions is property. Just to buy and manage property you need to leverage brokers, conveyancers, commercial solicitors, banks, private lenders, joint-venture partners, commercial lenders, agents, builders, letting agents, estate agents, refurbishment teams, business advisors, millionaires and billionaires, tax specialists, accountants, business partners and employees, specialist consultants (marketing, PR, sales, design, tech, etc.) ...

You don't have all the answers and all the knowledge on your own. The Life Leverage philosophy is about getting the best possible network you can, because it is your path of least resistance and least effort to maximum results. They've been there and done it. They've had all of the problems and pain, and have solved them and grown to a higher level. If you're smart, you get to leverage all of that. It is not clever to keep going through that process yourself in the name of 'learning on the job' or 'saving on courses and mentors'.

As an artist (when I was skint and unhappy), I wanted to trailblaze. I never went to any galleries or looked at other artists' work because I wanted to be unique and special. What an ignorant idiot I was! We are all influenced by others all the time, and that's OK; it's called inspiration. Musicians were inspired by musicians they loved to listen to, Rory McIlroy was inspired by Tiger Woods, comedians were inspired by laughing at their favourite stand-ups. But no, I wanted to be unique. I hated conceptual and installation art. I considered it to be a joke. Damien Hurst cutting up dead animals and Tracey Emin unmaking beds to me were ridiculous. But they were rich and I was bitter.

If I had the choice between being bitter and traditional or modern and rich, I know which one I'd choose now, every single time. Tracey Emin is a CBE thanks to her art and I was a nobody. Damien Hurst's net worth is reputedly between £240 million and £700 million thanks to art and I made about 14 pence in three years before tax. Damien Hirst sold 1,365 of his spot paintings (which, incidentally, he leveraged his company/workshop to do), while I have half of my paintings still hanging in my house because I couldn't sell them. Damien Hirst and Tracey Emin served more people than me. I could have and should have learned from them and the many great artists like them and before them.

YOUR HIGHEST KRA?

Building and investing in your 'mastermind network' or peers, coaches, mentors and specialists should be one of your highest KRAs. Many of your IGTs will and should focus on your mastermind network. The Life Leverage way is to get someone else to do it:

- To get someone better to do it

- To get the best to do it

- To get someone who's been through all the mistakes before to (help you) do it

- To have guidance, support, encouragement (and tough love) to do it.

And you can count the money. Spend at least one-third of your 'work' time 'working' on your network.

There are five ways you can leverage someone's knowledge or experience. You want to be doing all of these:

- Networking

- Receiving positive peer pressure

- Role modelling

- Mentoring

- Masterminding.

Let's look at each one.

NETWORKING

This is not rocket science so I won't patronize you. But could you get out there and meet more smart people? Sure you could. Could you be strategic and get yourself out cherry-picking the events where wealthy and successful people hang out? Of course you can. Charity balls, business angel events, flying clubs, high-end gyms, golf clubs, Rotary clubs, sailing clubs, boat shows, business and property expos, property or business networking events: there are many places where you can rub shoulders with wealthy and successful people.

> 'The secret that smart people know is the smart people they know.'
> – Rob Moore

Your access to finance, your extended bank account, is the extent of your network. Because no one starts with money, and to get money it has to be exchanged from one person to another, money has less to do with how much you have in the bank and more to do with how much your network has access to. Your relationship with that network is the mechanism of fair exchange. If you have a wealthy extended network, and a trusted relationship with that network, you have fair exchange and money will flow your way.

RECEIVING POSITIVE PEER PRESSURE

Peer pressure is mostly seen as the negative influence that others can have to drag us down. But it can work in a positive way, too. If the people are influencing and 'pressurizing' you to a higher level of challenge, growth and being, then you want it. It can feel uncomfortable and out of your comfort zone to be in the presence of greatness and vast wealth, but the person who gets the most benefit from an interaction is the poorest person in the room.

Positive peer pressure is one of the genuine little-known secrets to wealth and success, probably the quickest 'shortcut' that isn't a scam or get-rich-quick scheme, and it's the Life Leverage philosophy in action. You get forced up to a higher level of success through association, which, although challenging, is one of the easiest routes to success.

ROLE MODELLING

Strategically seek out people who've got the lifestyle you want and wine, dine, interview, grill and stalk them. Analyse their rituals, habits and behaviours. Tap into their already leveraged network for double leverage. The people who were once your idols will become your peers, friends and business partners.

If you want specific knowledge in specific areas, ask the most knowledgeable for some tips and summaries. Each time there is a significant change in the economy that could affect the property market, I'll let my business partner and finance expert, Mark Homer, author of the best-selling book *Low Cost High Life*, do all the analysis and research, and then ask for his summaries, opinions and predictions. I'll even let him do most of the worrying for me if it is a challenging change, and outsource most of that the Life Leverage way.

MENTORING

I don't know of a successful sports- or businessperson who hasn't had (multiple) coaches and mentors. All the answers are everywhere, and someone before you has already done what you want to do. You can learn from your own niche or industry, or from different fields. You can have personal paid coaches, successful business mentors, 'free' peer groups or paid-for masterminds, and you can study and read up on successful people and enterprises.

One of the most valuable hobbies/studies I've added to my life over the last decade is reading biographies and autobiographies. You get great insights into companies, sportspeople and leaders in their field – their ethos, behaviours, life tips, insights and strategies. You can be a fly on the wall of greatness, like the passage in Steve Jobs' autobiography where he and Bill Gates meet and chat quite soon before Jobs' death.

Or where Arnold Schwarzenegger gives you his top tips in life and success at the end of his autobiography, *Total Recall*. It's like being there receiving secrets to success in the company of greatness. It is even better to be able to get these experiences and insights face to face, and one of your continued life KRAs should be to constantly seek out great people for peers and mentors. It really is one of the simplest ways to create maximum leverage, gaining from their entire life experiences in far less time and with far less wastage. This has made a huge difference in my life, one of the main reasons why life is so much better now, and something I just can't understand that I didn't understand before. If I'd have known this when I was 18, I'd have been dangerous!

MASTERMINDING

A mastermind is a collective of 'master minds' – smart people who get together to help one another, combining unique and complimentary skills that are more powerful as a whole.

I am a member of many mastermind groups as a mentor and as a peer, and wouldn't see business as functioning properly without them. You get some of the biggest insights, benefits and strategic direction from putting great minds together and letting them create solutions and solve problems. Someone 'around the table' or in the group has the answer, a new or different way of looking at the challenge, or knows someone who can help. You don't know to ask the questions you didn't know to ask, so you get as much benefit from being a 'voyeur' on other people's business discussions, whether in the same industry as yours or a different one, where you can often borrow innovations for your own niche. And you often learn as much from being the mentor as you do from being the mentee.

For personal and company progress, and the progress of our community, we make strategic decisions every year to both run and be part of master-mind collectives as mentors and as peers. One of my companies, Progressive Property, runs the UK's largest, yet most personal, property mastermind

– the 12-month Progressive VIP Programme, a mentoring, support, account-ability and private finance property investors' network – and the Cayman Legacy, where five millionaires mastermind eight to ten high-level business-people to a national or global vision and six-, seven- and eight-figure results.

We sit as peers/students in two mastermind groups, one set up by us locally for fellow business owners to mastermind business and help with one other's challenges. Another, called 'The Syndicate', set up by a friend, where again a group of millionaires spend one day a quarter getting together and helping to solve one other's high-level business challenges. These are the most vital, high-level forms of networks that make the biggest difference to the inspiration, vision and results of the business and property empire you are building.

Many of the fellow mastermind members in groups we peer in and groups we mentor in become great friends and partners, with small ideas and distinctions making many millions of pounds and a greater difference. Having mentors in your mastermind will accelerate your results. Mentors are those who've been there and done it, are still doing it, and can guide you through the path of least resistance. Without mentors, I would be stuck with a dozen houses or so, at a much smaller scale, with a longer, harder journey. After initially being a bit tight, and looking for as much free help as I could get, one of my mentors pointed out that 'free advice is worth every penny'.

While you might not be able to afford mentors at the very highest level, you should target mentors at as high a level as possible, because you get what you pay for. Having great mentors is one of the best invest-ments you can make, and ignorance is very expensive.

Relationships, masterminds, mentors and extended networks are the highest form of leverage, even higher leverage than money, to help you to your goals, vision, making money and making a lasting difference.

Summary

Your network is your net worth, and the relationships you build are key to long and lasting growth and success. You cannot be an expert in all aspects of your business, so you must leverage as much as you can, getting people who are better at tasks to carry them out for you. Seek out people who you aspire to be like and learn from them. Get a mentor and a role model to accelerate your progress. Carefully select mastermind groups of peers and more experienced businesspeople to help you to learn more quickly, from people in the know. These groups are a great point of reference to help solve problems as well as to hold you accountable. The secret that smart people know is the smart people they know.

#15 Life Leverage leadership and management

Leadership and management are not the same, but they serve each other. If you are too busy managing, you can't lead, but if you don't have management teams and systems in place you can't do either. So they dovetail, fit hand in glove, are yin and yang, and any other clichéd analogy you can think of.

> 'Leaders are people who do the right thing;
> managers are people who do things right.'
> – Professor Warren G. Bennis

The Life Leverage definition of leadership is 'a process of social inspiration and influence, which brings together and maximizes the efforts of others, towards the achievement of a worthy goal'.

> 'Leadership is the art of getting someone else to do
> something you want done because he wants to do it.'
> – Dwight D. Eisenhower

Leaders set direction, build an inspiring vision, and create something new and worthwhile that people believe in, to serve their own vision and values. They build and guide the best team to achieve that vision. It's the easiest hard work in the world, and if you could choose a 'job' or career that encapsulated the Life Leverage philosophy best, it would be leadership. The great news is that you can be a leader in any niche or vocation you choose. Yet, while leaders set the direction, they must also use basic management skills and hire and leverage great managers to guide their people to the right destination, in an efficient and effective way.

LIFE LEVERAGE LEADERSHIP

Here are the 80/20, Life Leverage philosophies you want to develop and own to be a great leader and get more done in less time, outsource everything and create a mobile lifestyle:

1. Vision

2. Team building

3. Inspiration

4. Feedback.

Let's look at each one.

1. Vision

You sell and share your life vision, break it down into the project vision and link it to how it serves the values and vision of the individuals in the team. Set a clear defined outcome and destination of the project that is tangible and achievable – the vision coming into reality.

2. Team building

As the leader, you are responsible for building the very best team you possibly can. Maximum results and maximum time preservation are dependent on this. Steve Jobs was (in)famous for pinching the very best people in and out of Apple at key stages, whether hiring the head of Pepsi or working on a silo or solo project within the company. The best football managers are known to bring their backroom staff of assistant managers, physios and statisticians with them when they are hired at a new football club.

You are only as good as your team, and you can only live the Life Leverage way with a great team around you. The plethora of publications promoting life on a beach on your laptop sipping piña coladas with no staff is a fantasy of lazy or deluded idealists who think they can do no work, add no value, be responsible for no one and still make millions. Nobody ever succeeded to a significant level, or served many people and made a real difference, on their own.

I remember having a peaceful coffee at my local café, when a woman recognized me and asked me how many staff we had at Progressive now as she'd witnessed us growing and remembered when we were a two-man-band start-up. I told her the number, around 40 at the time, and she spat her mocha out in amazement. 'Wow! How do you sleep at night with 40 staff?' she blurted.

'Because we have 40 staff,' I said, confused.

To her, staff were problems, overheads and a constant babysitting responsibility. It reminded me of one of my dad's revelations about business in his tougher years as a pub landlord: 'Son, the two worst things about business are the staff and the customers!'

Most self-employed people end up with this cynical view. You have a certain naive idealism when you start your business, which is probably a good thing or you'd never even start it. As you grow as an entrepreneur, your skills and focus need to grow, too. You start to do everything yourself in the name of keeping costs down and getting it off the ground as quickly as possible. That same mentality and ethic that built your business so quickly from nothing to something is actually the single biggest block to growth once you have built the foundations of your business. This is why most entrepreneurs fail or have visions of being business owners but are in fact glorified employees reporting to themselves and slaves to their self-sabotaging venture.

Vision, people and systems are the three mechanisms for growth. Since people perform tasks towards your vision and operate systems, you could say that people (the team) are the single biggest factor in growth, scale and vast service.

I'm frequently asked, 'Rob, if you could start over again, what would you do differently?' Well, at the time of writing we've generated well in excess of £30 million, doing what we love and loving what we do, so why would I do anything differently?

But here's what I'd work on earlier, faster and focus much more time on: leverage, people and vision.

I would spend less time working 'hard hard hard' with no real direction, and more time on vision, strategy and hiring. And I would hire the key people for growth such as a personal assistant or finance director much earlier, even before I thought I could afford it. Finding great people would have freed up my time to do what I am best at, leveraged what I am worst at, and build more compounded momentum. Instead of waiting for everything to break before we looked at spending any more on people, we could have had them for three to six months, ready and inspired, by the time we needed them.

A big mistake entrepreneurs or human resources people often make is unconsciously hiring a stereotype. I've seen it a lot. In my early endeavours in business I'd always been attracted to and hired people who were just like me three years ago. Unproven and passionate. Raw but hardworking. This turned out to be great for one to two years, but this type of person never seemed to stay long enough. Ironically (or logically), I did exactly the same thing before setting up Progressive: I worked long, hard and passionately for someone for about a year, then burned and blew out.

This is the *wrong* way to hire. But unless they are experienced in recruiting, this is what most people do because we like what we like, and we don't what we don't. We see the vision of the world through our own distorted reality as if it is real and the only reality. We are all therefore delusional.

The best way to hire is as follows:

- Be very clear on the role, KRAs and job description.

- Be very clear on the type of person you want, and don't want.

- Do not hire the same type of person as you; hire for the role.

- Strategically, look to build a team of apparent misfits, a variety of types of people and polarized skills and specialities, and appreciate what their creative differences will bring.

Radiohead, possibly the most creative and innovative band of all time regardless of personal taste, had many 'creative arguments' when writing albums. Thom Yorke, the lead singer, had both traditional and modernist influences, and Jonny Greenwood, the lead guitarist, had very classical and technical skills and roots. They often disagreed as band members, to the point of falling out sometimes. Thom often wanted to move away from the albums that were most popular and other band members wanted to do more of the same old formula. There's no doubt in my mind that this 'creative tension' and respect for their differences created their experimentation and innovation.

You want your team to be like a band – each member technically great at their own individual instrument, all with different personalities and influences. The frontman and drummer cannot take the same role, but both are just as important to the overall symphony. In fact, while the frontman might get all the celebrity and glory, the drummer leads the song with the consistent beat. Sometimes bass plays lead, sometimes you have a three- or a five- or even a nine-piece, like Slipknot. Sometimes you have an epic solo but you always have the band: a greater sum than the parts.

The Life Leverage philosophy of team building is to outsource or joint venture all your weaknesses and hates. It liberates you from what holds you back, so you can forge forward and do more of what you love and what you are great at. This is the ideal in life that most aspire to, but their weaknesses always catch up with them and hold them back. The solution is to outsource and leverage virtually all of them aside from leadership. Develop your leadership skills, especially your greatest strength and biggest flaw in leadership, and outsource, leverage, hire and inspire the rest.

3. Inspiration

Create your vision. Sell it and share it. Lead people along it to the predetermined destination. Care about the team and the individuals enough to find out their values and take them on a journey that meets their values through your vision. False or transient pumped-up motivation is not the same as inspiration.

4. Feedback

Feedback is the mechanism that checks that everything is moving in the right direction, for the entire team, not just the leader. You may be doing something the wrong way or the long way. You may be going in the wrong direction or no direction. You may think you're flying but the team are dying. Feedback is the way back.

Feedback in all directions, which means you as the leader have to accept, embrace and invite it too, is the only way to accurately evaluate the progress towards your vision. Never let your ego get in the way of vital and valuable information that could correct your course, solve a problem or serve the greatest number of people.

LIFE LEVERAGE MANAGEMENT

Leaders set and inspire a team towards a vision. Managers hold their hand, guide them, support them and help them operationally and logistically get there.

Here are the 80/20 Life Leverage philosophies you want to develop and systemize to create effective management structures and get more done in less time, outsource everything and create a mobile lifestyle:

1. Share your vision and inspiration.

2. Have a manager to manage the managers and the team.

3. Set the course; adjust the course.

4. Let them get on with it.

5. Give good feedback.

Let's look at each one in detail.

1. Share your vision and inspiration.

People need to feel that they are working towards something worthwhile. Progress towards a worthy goal is scientist David Lieberman's key finding of happiness. Vision is very much at the core of the Life Leverage philosophy. As the leader/manager, you are the source of the vision, and the inspiration to the team that you can get there together. This is possibly your highest KRA as a leader. Refocusing on the vision will solve many of the issues and challenges that arise on your journey.

2. Have a manager to manage the managers and team.

The bigger your team gets, the harder it is to manage and spread your inspiration across everyone. According to many management experts, six or seven people is the maximum that any individual should directly manage. Any more and the workload, pressure and overwhelm increase and the ability to be effective and to give care and attention diminishes.

As you get out of operations and into management, you will encounter new challenges. Your open-door policy needs to close and, instead of saying, 'Ask me any time', you need to say 'Ask someone else.' This creates a cultural change. You can't make the difference you once made yourself because you can't be everywhere at once, and people who were close to you will start to feel disconnected and shut out. You need to set new boundaries where you lead them more but help and support them less. You now teach them to find their own answers, solve their own problems and go to someone else for the support. If that person is a new manager, that can cause conflict and rejection.

While you are going through this growth, some of your team will grow and some will go. You will need to grow through it too, letting go more, accepting more mistakes you could have solved, seeing a longer-term vision and accepting short-term pains that could have been avoided (like handing over sales to a salesperson where there is an initial dip in sales or where some customers only want to deal with the owner of the business). Micro-management goes to macro-management goes to outsource the management. Ask for suggestions, not questions. Trust them to solve problems and challenges, and give them enough space, autonomy and respect to give it their best shot. Let them start now and get perfect later.

3. Set the course; adjust the course.

An aircraft using a satellite navigation system is off course much more frequently than it is on course. This excerpt from jsgilbert.com explains an aircraft's journey and destination:

'The plane does have a course heading that it follows, but on average, any airplane will actually be off course for 95 per cent of its flight. The computers on board will tell the plane that it has veered 5 degrees off course due south, for example. Sophisticated systems then allow the plane to make a correction. As the plane corrects, factors such as wind now may place the plane off course by a few degrees southwest, and once again the plane makes a correction. This continues for the entire flight.

'Thus, we see that, for a plane to get from New York to Los Angeles, it requires an ability to constantly evaluate its position (relative to where it might want to be) and be able to make necessary corrections. Instruments work well, but the airplane requires a good pilot. The pilot is able to listen for instructions from various sources, as well as scan the skies for additional information that then help the plane further in its never-ending quest to correct itself.

'Additional factors, related to weather, national security or migrating birds may pose challenges to the plane, and it will be required to take this additional input into account to allow it to make best choices for correcting. In many cases, the plane must abandon its flight path altogether, occasionally causing it to venture out into unknown territories, often due to unforeseen circumstances.

'The plane may change course to avoid potential problems, or it may accept a different course because it is taking advantage of a jet stream or some other opportunity.'

And so it is with leadership and management. This is your role and a very high KRA and IGT.

4. Let them get on with it.

Sell them the vision, give them the team, resources and autonomy, set the timeline and let them get on with it. Resist all urges to fiddle or stick your nose in, as hard as you may find it, even if you feel they are getting it wrong. You hired them or got them involved in the first place, to show your faith and trust in them. They could surprise you, and your ability to grow is dependent on their ability to grow.

5. Give good feedback.

The right environment for changes, ideas and solutions is through controlled feedback and mentoring. Feedback should never be ripping someone's head off and tearing into them, especially not publicly. Over-emotionally fuelled 'feedback' will always lose more than it gains, and build bad blood that will cost you time, money, staff and customers.

This is perhaps one of the biggest challenges for a passionate, 'wearing your heart on your sleeve' entrepreneur. You expect everyone to work as hard as you and care as much as you. But you can't judge people by your own standards because people will only ever live up to their own. Control your emotions, store and save the feedback, and give it in the right, controlled environment such as a briefing or debrief meeting or one to one.

And, perhaps hardest of all, you have to encourage feedback on yourself and your methods, and be humble and smart enough to listen, accept and consider it. If you don't take feedback on, why should anyone listen to you?

Master this and you will go far. Master business and you will master life.

LIFE LEVERAGE MANAGEMENT 'HACKS'

Here are some techniques you can use to implement the Life Leverage philosophy into your management and leadership:

1. Find out key team members' values.

Care enough about your team to find out what is most important to them, using the questionnaire we looked at in Chapter 11, 'What is most important to you in your life?' Armed with this knowledge, you have vital unique information on what motivates and inspires each person, and you can sell your overall vision or operational task based on what is most important to them, by either giving them tasks that meet their values or linking how doing what you want them to do will serve their highest values.

2. Running projects

If you order people around and leverage your authority, even if you wrap it in candyfloss, people will build resentment towards you. They begrudgingly perform the task, secretly hoping it will go wrong, and give a limp half-attempt at getting it done – late and badly.

A more elegant and sustainable way is to have your team involved in the creation and planning process, having their say, being part of building it and owning a little bit of the project. They'll own the hard work, long hours and tight deadlines, and will have the same aligned vision and outcome as you.

So follow this process:

- **Give them autonomy.**

Give them trust and responsibility. Let them crack on. Trust them to lead.

- **Have them feel they came up with the idea.**

Suggestions before instructions. Draw out the great ideas you want to impart and give the ownership to the team.

- **Have their suggestion and buy-in for deadlines.**

People hate what they perceive to be unrealistic deadlines. If you extract from them the time frame, maybe even give them a few days on top, they will own it and are far more likely to hit it.

- **Have chunked-down short meetings to catch up.**

Have short regular check-ins and catch-ups, not long drawn-out meetings. Like the aircraft, keep evaluating the direction rather than wait to be miles off course.

- **Ensure reporting and KPIs throughout the process (weekly, monthly).**

Keep checking the data. Tweak accordingly.

- **Have one person responsible for the overall project.**

Yes, it is a team game, but more than one person, or no one, being responsible means that everyone has an excuse or a scapegoat. One person has to lead, not to be the fall guy but to create ownership, direction and management.

3. Running meetings

Meetings either don't happen enough and no one knows what anyone else is doing, or occur too often and go on soooooooo long that there seem to be meetings about meetings about meetings.

Here's how to run them the Life Leverage way:

- **Always have a clear outcome for the meeting.**

You need one sentence on what the meeting is to achieve. Have the outcome and the points broken into an agenda sent out before the meeting so that there is time for everyone to prepare.

- **Have clear, short agenda points.**

Between three and seven short agenda points should be sent out before the meeting. Keep them clear and concise and avoid overwhelm.

- **Have a predetermined timeline for the meeting.**

Set the time allowed for the meeting beforehand. Do not let it drag out. Keep the meeting moving forward. Let one person lead it and stop the digressions. Have someone remind you ten, five and two minutes before the end, and if it still isn't finished, finish it anyway and rebook for the rest. This should soon teach you to match the agenda with the allotted time.

- **Set actions and deadlines and take minutes.**

At least one person should take full notes. Action steps and who owns them should be set throughout the meeting. Minutes are then sent out immediately afterwards with notes and actions. These are then reviewed in the next meeting. What was done, not done, and why?

4. Managing email

Email, while one of the most important innovations of the twentieth century, can be the bane of everyone's life. Later in *Life Leverage* I will share a very clever, simple and effective email management system to keep your inbox empty, no matter how many emails you get.

For now, here are some email management techniques:

- ### Email, phone call or face to face?

Sometimes people waste an hour in a meeting when one email would have said it. Other times there are reams of threads and multiple people copied in and you seem to go around in circles, when five minutes, face to face would clear it all up. The skill is knowing when to email, when to talk on the phone, and when to meet face to face. Don't ever hit 'Send' when you want to shoot someone in the face. Don't put anything in an email you wouldn't feel happy sending to a newspaper. Don't fire anyone on email.

- ### The 'To' field in emails

I almost can't believe I'm writing this point, because it seems so small and trivial. I receive many emails with six people addressed in the 'To' field, and I have no idea whom it is actually addressed to, and who is being asked to respond. So no one does. Whoever you are addressing specifically, or is responsible and accountable, put their address in the 'To' field. Put all others in the 'Cc' field. Never embarrass or fire a rocket at anyone while anyone else is directly copied in, unless its for a very strategic reason, so copy someone in the 'Bcc' instead. Ensure that the thread of emails is continued when replying but never forward anything sensitive (which we've all done and wished there was an 'Unsend' button!).

Summary

Build a team. Learn to be a great leader. Hold people to a higher standard than they hold themselves to. Use all the resources you have, not just money, to get other people working towards your vision. 'Do' less yourself, and 'leverage' and 'inspire' more. Spend more time thinking and less time being busy. Seek feedback, continually tweaking your vision and strategy and you will make a lasting difference.

#16 Letting go and saying 'No'

One of my mentors once said to me, 'Rob, what got you here won't get you there.' Albert Einstein, who would have been an amazing mentor, said, 'We cannot solve our problems with the same thinking we used when we created them.'

I think this sums up the entrepreneurial journey. There are many stages, and the only constant is change. What urges you to start up, and the hard-work-DIY nature of getting your enterprise off the ground, has to change in order for the enterprise to grow. If it, and you, don't evolve, the business will decay. I suppose it is natural and normal for entrepreneurs to struggle to grow their business, because it demands perennial change, which for most isn't easy. However, if you can see growth as the outcome, growth as success, then you can have continual progress to a worthy goal. Your enterprise can continue to solve its own challenges through growth, and meet your own vision and values.

One of the key learnable skills is letting go.

In 2013, according to usatoday.com, Walmart had 2.2 million employees. Sam Walton could not manage them all himself, overseeing all-important decisions, doing everyone's one-to-ones each month. It's clear he's had to trust key people to fly the flag and live the values of Walmart, and he's relied on many people to grow his enterprise. The Arcadia Group, started by self-made UK entrepreneur Philip Green, has 44,000 staff according to wikipedia.org, which is the result of a personal loan of £20,000 to start his clothing business. Almost every entrepreneur I've met or taught or spoken in front of (it's in the hundreds of thousands) is about to, has to, is going through or is a victim of letting go. It's one of the biggest barriers to success. Master it and the enterprise grows; fail at it and the enterprise slows or goes.

Most entrepreneurs think they are alone in this dichotomy. In the thick of it they doubt they can do it, convincing themselves that their customers want and need them personally, that no one cares about their business as much as they do, and that no one else can do as good a job. This is the big delusion. It's the dip or growing pains that are feared, and the breakage, loss of customers and potential drop in income perceived that keeps them operating like a one-man band – the antithesis, in short, of the Life Leverage philosophy.

Here's the good news: every enterprise of any scale beyond the owner has gone through this exact growing pain and transition. It's a learnable skill, and you can get out of your own way and learn and grow through the challenges. When Steve Jobs died, I really thought Apple would struggle to rule the world in the way they had, because I couldn't see that his leadership and inspiration were going to be matched by anyone else. So far, I have been proved wrong. Perhaps it's just the gargantuan momentum or addiction and pain of disconnect that have kept customers loyal fans, or perhaps Steve Jobs really did have his values transfused into key members of the team so they could continue to grow. Only time will tell but there seem to be no cracks, at last on the outside, and I'm sitting here writing this on a Mac, listening to music downloaded from iTunes, and running my life from my iPhone.

Here are the Life Leverage philosophies of letting go and saying 'No':

1. Have a vision and a plan of what growth looks like.

2. Accept some fallout.

3. Hire great people.

4. Compartmentalize growth KRAs and IGTs.

5. Measure your progress.

1. Have a vision and a plan of what growth looks like.

Start by putting growth high on your KRAs and IGTs. Spend more time on this vision and strategy than on operations. Focus on growth in the form of getting out of day-to-day operations, hiring a personal assistant, managing director and other key managers and 'managing the change'.

What's the vision? What's the time frame? What does the organizational chart look like once you have achieved the vision? What systems do you need? What training of the team needs to happen?

Keep checking and evaluating your vision and progress towards it against your VVKIKs.

2. Accept some fallout.

There will be attrition. You will lose some customers. You may lose some key team members who are set into the old ways. Things will break. It's a lot like splitting up with an unstable ex-partner. You avoid it because you know they will flip out, it gets worse and worse and worse, you finally pluck up the courage to end it, they flip out anyway, it hurts for a while, then you are relieved, and then you wish you'd done it way sooner. The sooner you start, the sooner you will be out of day-to-day operations and able to fully live the Life Leverage philosophy.

'Let bad small things happen so big good things can happen' is a quote I found on Facebook but can't track its origin.

3. Hire great people.

If you hire great people, the risk of breakage upon handover is greatly reduced. It will be easier to let them get on with it, let things go, accept the odd mistake, and make strategic transition as smooth as it can be. You are in control of your hiring process, so in theory you should be able to control the fallout from growth.

Trust is the single biggest factor in letting people carry the torch of your business operations. If you have trust in them, you won't meddle and fiddle. Micro-management is one of the proven biggest demotivators for team members. I find that if you trust people, even before they have really earned it, the likelihood of them living up to and into that 'faith of trust' increases. And if you don't trust them, why did you hire them in the first place? Replace them fast.

In order to gain control of your life, you need to let go of control of parts of your business that at one stage you never thought you would, could or should. Operations such as someone else selling your products and services (and not you), someone having access to your bank account and paying invoices (and not you), and someone else having access to your database and marketing to your customer list (and not you) fit this description. It is a real sign of growth and progress when you can grow through and leverage out key functions such as these, and in order to do that you need great people whom you can trust, and you need to get out of the way and let them do it.

Start small, let trust, training and capability grow and be earned. At first, give financial people controlled access to bank accounts with set limits and restrictions on maximum amounts that can be paid out by them. Allow team members to sign off invoices to be paid under a certain amount at first, with you signing off the bigger ones, and gradually increase this as trust increases. Give your first salesperson lots of training and a few colder leads at the start before you hand over your big accounts. Think big, start small and focus on the vision.

4. Compartmentalize growth KRAs and IGTs.

The dichotomy of letting go and saying 'No' is that you need to train other people to take over, but you're too busy doing those very tasks to train people to take them over. And so it is that most entrepreneurs default back to working hard and *in* the business, not smart and *on* the business. The single, most effective way to grow through this change and handle both strategy and operations while you are transitioning is to compartmentalize the time. We will look at this in the next chapter.

Make sure you put evergreen, non-negotiable 'Do not remove', 'Do not delete' time into your weekly diary, specifically for vision, strategy and training. You should do this always but, for the purpose of this chapter, for the specific outcome of coaching, training, supporting and giving feedback to the key people you are grooming for key positions that will help you grow and let go. If you hire them and are too busy to help them, you will create more of a mess. But if you don't prioritize and compartmentalize time, you will naturally fill it with operational stuff to save short-term breakages or take the low-hanging fruit of money or the easier road. If you're too busy to coach, train, support and feed back, you are too busy to grow and scale.

5. Measure your progress.

How do you know if you are making progress through letting go and saying 'No'? How do you know if your team are coping with or even embracing the change? The only way is to measure, and measurement comes from KPIs and seeking feedback.

Many one-man-band self-employed people, who think they are entre-preneurs, have the attitude that they know their business and/or affairs better than anyone else. This is either through fear of making mistakes, looking weak or vulnerable in front of others, or a more arrogant 'What do underlings know about my business?' Real entrepreneurs and business owners who want to make a real difference don't take this insular, complacent or, worse, would-be omnipotent view. They ask, listen and tweak accordingly.

The title and subtitle of this book came from questions and surveys posted to communities I'm involved in. After many suggestions and variations, what was settled on, 'Life Leverage: How to get more done in less time, outsource everything and create your ideal mobile lifestyle', was favoured by a great majority. So by common sense this book is likely to be bought by the most people it can, and to help them, too. It wasn't my personal first choice, and wasn't even something I can say I came up with directly; it's more the result of continual feedback. As I want to help the most people and make the biggest difference, it felt like the right and only way to create the book. In fact, I'd be an idiot to have given it any other title. Much of the content of this book has been created from observing the challenges my communities have, and serving and solving for them.

Sometimes you don't know you're going wrong.

Sometimes you don't know what you don't know.

Sometimes you've never done it before.

Feedback has been a recurrent theme in serving, solving and scaling using the Life Leverage philosophy. Feedback from mentors who've been there can make a huge difference. Feedback from those on the ground, more connected to the reality and operations, can make a huge difference. You can't be expected to know everything or always have the right answer. Many people feel responsible for having all the answers as a leader, but I believe that is delusional and not their role. Their role is to care enough about the team members to involve them in the vision. The more feedback you get from team members, the more the sum of the ideas is greater than the individual parts, and the more part of the vision they feel.

Even criticism, fair but harsh, is valuable to you. Once you get over yourself you may have just been given vital information for you to grow. All answers are there and everywhere. Often, you just have to get out of your own way, not take it personally and see it as valuable insight in adjusting your strategy to get closer to your vision. Not everything is worth implementing, but all feedback is worth considering and using as a measurement mechanism. Feedback is also a sign of a real leader. If people feel comfortable enough with and about you to give you feedback, you've likely created a nurturing environment. 'Feedback is the breakfast of champions,' they say. Now hurry up and get this book read – you're too slow, you lazy so-and-so!

THE CHALLENGES OF LETTING GO AND SAYING 'NO'

When you are growing, letting go and changing culture, tell people early in the process what you are doing, planning and get them involved in the vision. They will embrace and endure change and challenge much more if the path has been set and cleared, and you have honoured and cared for them enough to involve them in the process and given them time and respect to embrace the change.

Be honest that it won't all be easy. Some people may not like it (some may even leave), but explain that you truly believe that the new vision is the right thing to do to make the biggest difference.

Give people time. Don't expect everything to happen in five minutes. Have a fair and reasonable 'handover period' where you give time and training and accept some mistakes along the way. Be forgiving when people are learning and support them through change.

DEALING WITH CRITICS AND HATERS

Don't worry about what others say about your 'crazy, deluded vision'. Everyone will have something to say from afar about what you're doing and not doing. And if you think that kind of thing will go away the more successful you become, then get over that right away. Don't be naive. It will only get bigger. What other people think of you is none of your business. They don't know you, what you've gone through or the sacrifices you've made. Pandering to others' wants and criticisms, and focusing too much on other people's opinions, are guaranteed ways to be distracted from your vision. In fact, wear their comments and criticisms like a badge of honour. They never made statues of critics, and it is unlikely that you'll ever meet a hater doing better than you. Embrace critics along the way – they are part of the journey, there to help you grow and challenge you to continually feed back, learn and develop. Listen to what is a truth; bat off the rest.

SAYING 'NO'

Surprisingly, saying 'No' is very hard for many people. My dad used to run pubs and clubs, and he'd always tell me never to serve anyone who was really drunk. He'd tell me they would end up being trouble. And, despite him always being right, I usually didn't have the heart or courage to say 'No', would serve them a pint, and more often than not they'd spill it everywhere and upset the other customers. Dad would have to step in, kick them out (which he strangely enjoyed) and I would feel weak and stupid.

For many people like me, the inability to say 'No' is the source of much of their unhappiness, overwhelm, resentment and lack of self-worth. You can end up doing all manner of things for other people that you don't like and that take you away from your vision. You can juggle too many tasks in the hope of being seen as a martyr, only to do none of them well and to resent all the things you have going on and the people you said 'Yes' to.

Perhaps you fear what others will think or say of you if you say 'No'. Perhaps you are trying to avoid conflict. Perhaps you worry that they may feel rejected or that you really don't want to help people. Perhaps you see it as a weakness to say 'No'. Whichever one it is, be aware that none of these reasons is real, but just opinion, perception or delusion. There's nothing wrong with politely saying, 'Thank you for the opportunity. I am grateful and remember when no one would have asked me for any help. I would love to do it / help you, I just can't right now with all that I have on. Please keep me in mind for the future, though.' Not, 'Oh, OK then.'

How about 'Yes, but not today' or a polite 'Thank you, but this one isn't for me at this time'? If you feel busy, overwhelmed, stressed and out of control, remember that you created all the opportunities in your life. Only you. You created the workload. You created the responsibility. You created the 87,954 unread emails. So, if you want to uncreate them, start politely saying 'No'.

If you don't let go, you won't grow.

Summary

You can't grow if you don't let go of some or many of the tasks that you currently do yourself. You may think no one can do the job as well as you. But that's false. They can. You just need to find the right people and trust them to do the work that helps you towards your vision. Don't worry what critics might say about you. It doesn't matter. Chances are they are not doing better than you, so it doesn't matter what they think. Learning to say 'No' to people is absolutely necessary if you are going to grow. Say 'No' politely and firmly and you will eliminate the feelings of overwhelm and stress that block your vision and legacy. If you want to grow, you have to let go.

#17 Time compartmentalization

If you don't run your day, your day will run you. You've been there at 9 p.m. one night, having worked 14 hours and thought to yourself, 'What did I actually achieve today?' There's little more demoralizing than being really busy but getting nothing of any value done.

Remember, you can't manage time, you can only manage your life. So you could call 'time compartmentalization' 'life compartmentalization'.

Own the time you have and you will own your life.

Stop running around distracted all the time, worrying about what went wrong yesterday and what will go wrong tomorrow. Start blocking your time and your day into present-moment compartments.

DIARY MANAGEMENT

I don't know whether you run your diary like a military operation or don't even have one. My life would be an epic failure without a properly run diary. After ten years and many personal assistants who've resigned because of my chaos-ridden diary, here's what I've learned (we'll look at each in detail below):

1. Scrap it and redo it.

2. Synchronize your diary with important people and provide visibility.

3. Synchronize your diary across all your devices.

4. Block out most important time, first, one year ahead.

5. Block out most important time in your most productive time.

6. Use the recurring and invitee features.

7. Put enough detail and agendas in the 'notes' section.

8. Update/redo your diary every year.

Let's look at these now:

1. Scrap it and redo it.

A diary usually starts to look like an underground railway map after 12 months or so if used continually. At least once a year, ideally when the rest of the world is on shut-down (August, December), you should carry out a full cleanse of your diary, checking all recurring appointments and deleting all old or irrelevant entries. Clean out all devices, as some appointments will originate from different devices and still appear on some and not others (for example, on your Mac but not your phone, or in your diary but not your PA's).

Sit down with your life partner and check that the diary is in line and in balance with your family and social life. Do this at a similar time to doing your vision and goal setting, as these will link to each other. Check against your vision and KRAs. Check where you need to prioritize more time with loved ones, where you could merge vocation and vacation, and what you need to start doing, stop doing and keep doing.

2. Synchronize your diary with important people and provide visibility.

Ensure that your diary is accessible at home, at work, on your laptop, and on your mobile device. And make sure that the relevant people such as your PA, your business partner, key managers and your life partner have access to your diary. Get a techie you know to do it for you if the thought of doing it makes you nauseated. Once your diaries are synchronized and visible to the right people, they won't double-book you. They will learn your habits and movements and unconsciously learn when not to disturb you.

3. Synchronize your diary across all your devices.

Ensure that you can easily and quickly access your diary across all the devices you use, including your phone, laptop, home computer, work computer and tablet.

4. Block out most important time, first, one year ahead.

This is possibly the most important part of your diary (life) management. All VVKIK functions should be booked in first, before anything else, at least one year ahead. That includes family and social life as well as work, if there are separate functions. Sit down with your life partner and book in recurring, evergreen time compartments in your diary, and add 'DO NOT REMOVE' at the end.

These should be highly leveraged functions, or things you love to do the most, and could/should include:

- holidays (can you merge vocation with vacation?)

- date nights / nights in / time with loved ones / box-set marathons

- trips and excursions, school activities

- vision, strategy and planning time

- health, fitness or gym sessions or your important hobbies and passions

- meetings with key team members

- high-KRA functions

- leverage and outsourcing to others

- training and writing systems

- KPIs and reviews.

If these all get booked in, at least one year in advance, and are set to recur each week, month or year, then the rest of time, space and life will fit around it. If they don't, time, space and life will fill up and you will have no time left for any of the above, and you will feel overwhelmed, confused and frustrated. This is quite possibly one of the most leveraged functions that will create and free up the most amount of time with the maximum focus, minimum time wastage and fastest route to your vision.

5. Block out most important time in your most productive time.

Adding the Life Leverage philosophy to time compartmentalization, observe your daily energy and productivity cycles. When are you most productive, in flow and on fire? When does the carb-coma kick in and how long does it last? When do you like to be alone? When do you like to socialize? When do you prefer to work and when do you feel playful? When are you inspired?

I have studied and researched energy cycles. Some say that it's best to get up really early, but some like to work late. Some say you need a power nap in the middle of the day. Some say you need to eat light at lunch. Some say you need eight hours' sleep; others say you only need five. What is right?

What works for you, based on your habits, is what is right.

The problem is that most people aren't self-aware enough to link their energy and productivity cycles with their time and life management. For the next two weeks, keep a work and energy log. A simple document of notes will do: jot down hour by hour or when relevant what you did, when you worked and played, and how you felt about it. When were you in the zone? When was it a struggle? When did you feel productive? You will get amazing insight into your daily cycles and routines, and you can set yourself up for maximum results with minimum time wastage by aligning your diary with your daily cycles and habits.

Put all high-KRA functions in the time you're in flow. Put any administration and non-important/urgent tasks in your crash-and-burn time. Put KRAs and IGTs in the diary when you know you can be alone and get things done. Book your holidays well in advance around school holidays and when you feel at your lowest 'SAD' (seasonal effective disorder) point in the year. Eat when you are hungry, not just because lunch is 12:00 to 1:00 in everyone else's life.

Give me your thoughts, feedback and let me hold you accountable to your work and productivity log here:

www.facebook.com/robmooreprogressive

Now you can live an inspired life by your own standards that work the best for you. No more guilt or comparing yourself with others. No more conflict between task and energy, just getting more done in less time and creating your ideal mobile lifestyle.

For an idea to help you redesign your life this way, here are some epiphanies I've had over the years. Some of these may work for you, some may not, but at least you will have a blueprint guide to help you create your own:

- My most productive time: 5:45 to 8:30 a.m.

- Maximum efficient caffeine dosage: two coffees a day (any more and I turn into a passive-aggressive paranoid)

- Most creative time: 6:30 to 8:30 a.m.

- Crash-and-burn time: 5:45 p.m. onwards

- Best time to eat: 9 a.m., 2 p.m., 6 p.m. (never later: never book a dinner beyond 7 p.m.; I'll be the worst company)

- Not even one alcoholic drink benefits me, even if at the time I think it will. No need to drink. EVER.

- Best bedtime: 9 p.m. to 5:30 a.m.

- Best alarm clock: my son

- Worst time for meetings: 10:45 to 11:30 a.m. (lull before the second coffee of the day), therefore best time for unimportant admin that I'll probably not do but don't care

- Best time for Bobby's golf: 10 a.m., 3 p.m. or 5 p.m.

- Best time for gym: 8:30 a.m., 10 a.m. or 3 p.m.

- Most productive place to work: living room, café, anywhere with a nice view and Wi-Fi (not at the office)

- Best time to write this book: 4:30 to 8:30 a.m.

- Best time to send email instructions: before everyone gets to work

- Best time to catch up on emails / clear inbox: 6:15 to 8:15 a.m. or after 6 p.m. the night before

The point is, if you become self-aware, you can, by a factor of at least five, get more done in less time, enjoy your life, live the Life Leverage philosophy and make the biggest difference. Plan your day around you, strategically control your life and see 80/20 and compounding work for you, now!

6. Use the recurring and invitee features.

The recurring feature on the diary saves you from many important omissions, errors and oversights. It makes important functions evergreen. You can recur an appointment daily, weekly, monthly and/or yearly, safe in the knowledge that you'll never forget anything important. This works for VVKIK functions but also for renewing insurances, moving bank accounts to higher-interest ones, car servicing, birthdays and so on. Ensure that you book the recurrence enough time in advance of the deadline so you have time to meet it.

Invite all relevant or 'need to know' people into the diary entry. This can be the person responsible for the operation, the people who need to know what you are doing or the people who manage you, such as your PA, managing director or spouse.

7. Put enough detail and agendas in the 'notes' section.

'Meeting' is not enough detail or clarity for a meeting. If anyone invites me into a meeting and I am not 100-per-cent sure it will be clear when it comes up and I've long forgotten the origin, then it gets declined or deleted. Demand clarity about what the meeting is for, what the outcome is and what the specific agenda is.

8. Update/redo your diary every year.

Have a six- or 12-monthly review and cleanse of your diary to ensure maximum leverage of VVKIK.

BEING PRESENT IN THE MOMENT

Now that you have organized and compartmentalized your diary and aligned it with your energy and productivity cycles, you need to train yourself to be present in the moment, do the one main thing when you are diarized to do the one main thing, and block out absolutely everything else.

Performing a function while wishing, worrying or dwelling on a previous or future event will distract you from the moment, where all progress and happiness exists. You can only do what you can do now. You can only control what you can control now.

Here are some tools and techniques to help you with present moment focus:

- Just start now!

- Do one thing at a time – FOCUS.

- Stop interruptions and time drains.

Let's look at each of these in turn.

• Just start now!

Don't delay. Don't procrastinate. Don't make excuses. Start now. Get perfect later. Progression towards a worthy goal kicks out endorphins and serotonin (the chemicals in the brain that make you feel good), so starting a task will feel good, even if you only get a small way there. The Life Leverage philosophy for getting things done is to start now, get perfect later and tweak as you go.

• Do one thing at a time – FOCUS

FOCUS, if you remember, stands for 'Follow One Course Until Successful'. Focus for 30 to 90 minutes solidly on a single KRA or IGT, isolating yourself from all distractions, and rewarding your discipline with a mini-break. Do not task-jump from one thing to another every few minutes under the illusion that you are getting more done – you are just making yourself feel better than you are when, in fact, you are wasting time. Just as a cold car engine takes time to warm up, and a high-performance car will limit the revs and therefore speed you can go until it is completely warm, you get in-flow on a task after warming-up, not right away. Each time you chop, change and jump, you have to warm back up to the task again, and the constant warming-up is a time drain.

If you are smart, you can batch similar types of tasks together to mini-mize the warm-up phase and maximize the in-flow and FOCUS stage. You can run meetings back to back to back in one day: make sure you have everything you need on your laptop so you can get all tasks done without having to go back to the office, and so on.

• Stop interruptions and time drains.

Keep highly focused on your VVKIKs, and you will intuitively know what to do more of and what to drop. Isolate yourself with important KRA and IGT tasks so there is zero distraction. Don't even give temp-tation a chance, so that not even you can interrupt you! Get some big headphones so that you can look at people blankly when they talk to you.

Be aware of what the main time drains are, and completely avoid them. After a little research (outsourced to my researcher, of course) here are the amounts in percentages of total time typically wasted in a day:

- email: 40 per cent

- social media: 30 per cent

- phone notifications: 15 per cent

- surfing the Net: 5 per cent

- random errands: 10 per cent.

I could add a few: other people's problems, stop-start-stop-start-stop-start, arguments and debates. Ignore them all, especially other people's urgencies – people will always try to convince you that they are yours too. Evaluate the level of drama and urgency versus the reality of the situation and, if this is simply just their normal behaviour, send them to someone else.

Never answer your phone while in KRA or IGT time. If it is really urgent, the caller will find a way of finding you. Turn all dings and dongs and pings and noises off!

Summary

Don't let your day run you – run it! Managing your day and time in 'compartments' is extremely effective. Prioritizing according to your KRAs and IGTs, sharing your diary with those who matter and synchronizing all your devices will help you to time compartmentalize. Blocking out your most important time, such as time for family, exercise, vision and strategy should always come first. Understanding how and when you are most productive will increase your self-awareness and make you five times more effective. Duck out of all time drains. Productivity happens when dings and pings don't!

#18 NeTime

NeTime stands for 'No Extra Time'. It is a sweet little Life Leverage technique that maximizes time leverage and minimizes time wastage.

NeTime is getting multiple results for a single unit of time. It is not about juggling too many tasks, 'multi-tasking', spinning too many plates, or checking your phone while making sweet love, but where you can genuinely create a duplicate or triplicate result in a single amount of time.

Here are some NeTime functions:

- listening to programmes while travelling, exercising in the gym, walking …

- making calls while travelling (by train or car)

- watching autobiographical documentaries

- engaging with media while having a haircut at home

- getting the the train / a driver where possible and creating content/ work en route

- having a gardener, cleaner, cook, driver, nanny, maid

- merging a holiday with a business plan, vision, speaking engagement or mastermind

- merging shopping/trips with courses/events

- having dinner with mentors/businesspeople

- merging social events with business.

Let's look at each of these now.

- **Listening to programmes while travelling, exercising in the gym, walking …**

Never travel on a train or plane without educational audio in your headphones. This is the perfect opportunity for NeTime that literally buys back and frees up time. If you listen to audio, you free the time it would have taken to read, and you duplicate leverage from your gym, walk or travel.

If you did just one hour a day, that would be 3,650 hours every ten years.

The average university student studies for 13.9 hours per week, according to *The Guardian*. So one hour a day of audio, NeTimed on 2x speed, would be the same amount of time a university student works on their degree. You'd have the equivalent of three or four degrees every ten years, creating the time completely out of thin air because of NeTime leverage.

This year, from January to November, I have listened to 118 audiobooks, thanks to NeTime leverage on 2x speed. The average book is 3.5 hours long, so that is 413 hours of knowledge, education and inspiration that have been programmed into my brain, almost the equivalent of a three-year university degree.

- **Making calls while travelling (by train or car)**

Book all calls while travelling in the car or on the train so you preserve time duplication and get two things done in one unit of time. Don't accept any meetings on anyone else's time frame; only allow calls at certain times when you can NeTime. I tried this while at the gym but people thought I was a weirdo panting down the phone! If you NeTime and preserve just three hours a week, that's 6,240 hours over the next 40 years.

• Watching autobiographical documentaries

f you spend ten hours a week watching fictional TV, turn that into NeTime by watching educational and inspirational biographies and documentaries on Netflix, Apple TV and Sky.

• Engaging with media while having a haircut at home

You can save (and NeTime) up to three hours a month, by having a hairdresser come to your home or office to cut your hair. You save travel time to and from, and you can work on your phone while it is being cut (and blow-dried). I once conducted a meeting while having my hair cut in the office. The team thought that I thought I was some kind of Steve Jobs, but I don't care. NeTime leverage, baby! Assuming you have your hair cut once a month for the next 40 years, you preserve 1,440 hours.

• Getting the train / a driver where possible and creating content/work en route

A driver may cost £20 per hour, but if you NeTime and preserve three hours a week, that's 6,240 hours in 40 years. Unless you just gaze out of the window, using 80/20 Life Leverage you should be able to generate £100 revenue per hour from the £20 investment in the driver. Over the 40 years that's an extra £499,200.

• Getting a gardener, cleaner, cook, driver, nanny, maid

If each of the above cost you £20 per hour, and take, in total, 18 hours a week (not including driver), then you preserve for yourself and your life partner 37,440 hours in 40 years. Using 80/20 Life Leverage, if you generate £100 revenue from the £20 investment, that's an extra £2,995,200 using NeTime.

Add just these basic NeTime tasks up and you preserve £45,120. That's 1,880 days or 5.15 years over the next 40 years. Add up the extra NeTime revenue generation and you have an extra £3,609,600.

This stark comparison could be seen as unbelievable by some; it certainly will to the poor, because they don't know what they don't know.

Many people look at the wealthy and think they have all of the above 'luxuries' because they are rich. I would argue that they are rich because they invested in all these necessities.

These calculations rely on you being disciplined on IGTs with the time you replace the outsourced function with. Let's assume that you just had fun with 10,000 of the 45,120 hours you have preserved. Let's assume that you wasted another 10,000 and only generated a net gain of £10 for the remaining 25,120 hours. That is still a net gain of £251,200 over 40 years.

- **Merging a holiday with a business plan, vision, speaking engagement or mastermind**

NeTime your holiday time with business time to have a passion–profession, vocation–vacation merge. Rather than getting overwhelmed when you are working and horizontally detached when you are on holiday, achieve balance by not separating work and life. Earning while on holiday and holidaying while at work completely rewrites the rules the Life Leverage way, your way.

- **Merging shopping/trips with courses/events**

As above, turn shopping time into learning and earning time. Give yourself a nice treat while learning and earning and go on a little shopping spree. Don't spend all your earnings, though!

- **Having dinners with mentors/businesspeople**

If you're going to eat out, and it's not date night, mix business and pleasure by socializing with smart, interesting and experienced people who've done what you want to do and got what you want.

- **Merging social events with business**

Dining out with mentors or successful businesspeople is one of many ways to merge social and business. Learn to fly (I've met some amazing people at my local flying club), go to boat shows, charity balls, functions, business angel events; go anywhere where you can merge passion and profession.

One word of warning. If you use the word 'leverage' to your partner, they will soon throw that right back at your face. 'Leveraging' the dishes back to your partner will mean your only chance of getting any romance will be through leverage, too!

Summary

Getting multiple results in one single unit of time is what NeTime (or No Extra Time) is all about. Double or even triple up on tasks to get the most out of every minute of every day. Listen to audiobooks while you're on the train or in the gym, make phone calls while you're driving, get a cleaner, a nanny and a cook, merge holidays, dinners and social events with business and you will save valuable time. And make yourself a lot of money. Save up to five years over the next 40 years and make an extra £3,609,600 in revenue. It works.

Section 3: Tactics

In this section specific techniques, tools and systems will be detailed to enable you to systematically live Life Leverage. You will be given leverage and time/life management models, processes, acronyms and step-by-step templates. It helps to have easy-to-follow tools to fall back on when things start reverting back to the old ways. It helps with memory retention and habit creation. I'm not talking about how to number your to-do list, but about how to achieve the right balance between innovation that makes a difference quickly and tried-and-tested systems that aren't short-lived or a gimmick. You don't need another time management system that creates more work, I think you need Life Leverage tactics that help you get more done in less time, outsource everything and create your ideal mobile lifestyle.

#19 Priorities and posteriorities

KRAs and IGTs are your highest-priority tasks. Continual focus and feedback on your VVKIKs will ensure that you are instantly and intuitively doing the most leveraged task possible in any given moment.

Posteriorities are everything else. They are the lowest-value, most time-draining and most revenue-sucking tasks known to humankind: negative people, most emails, reunions and 'pity parties', most fictional TV (except *Suits*), selfies and foodies on social media, debates and arguments, gossip, mundane non-IGT administration; the list goes on.

Most people say procrastination is a bad thing, but procrastination is great on low-IGT tasks, known in Life Leverage as posteriorities. Be lazy, unmotivated, bored and apathetic in respect of all of these, and avoid or outsource. Doing these posteriorities and convincing yourself that you are working hard is no different from procrastination, other than it is active and takes ages. Beware of this self-delusion, which your split personality will try to convince you of. It is a liar. You are getting nowhere but, boy, does it take a long time to get there.

Parkinson's Law states that 'work expands so as to fill the time available for its completion'. If you don't prioritize and posterioritize, then all tasks become equal and fill the same amount of time and space. However, no two tasks are equal. Some take longer than others and some are more important than others. If you allow unimportant tasks to take priority over IGT tasks, they will fill all the time you have and there will be no space left to do the right, important and highest-leverage tasks. Therefore, high prioritization of KRAs and IGTs and ruthless procrastination of low-value tasks are essential for maximum productivity and Life Leverage.

Here are some techniques to distinguish priorities from posteriorities, and get more done in less time:

- Check your VVKIK focus and feedback loop.

- Revisit your vision and goals before bed and when you wake.

- Treat every day like the day before a holiday.

Here they are, one by one:

- **Check your VVKIK focus and feedback loop.**

The solution to lack of priority, overwhelm, confusion, lack of results and momentum and/or feelings of being a busy fool is always to check in against your vision, values, KRAs, IGTs and KPIs. If the task is high on the list, or gets you closer to your vision and enables you to live your values, do it. If not, delegate or dump it. Then keep checking in to ensure that you are on course and remove any confusion or procrastination.

- **Revisit your vision and goals before bed and when you wake.**

By reading your goals before you go to sleep and when you wake up, you're actually giving your brain and the neurological receptors of the unconscious mind instructional messages. This will command the unconscious to think about, solve and make things happen throughout the night and through the day. You will notice things and opportunities that you hadn't seen or thought of before, like a car you notice more when you become interested in or buy it.

Reading your goals before you go to sleep and when you wake up has shown to increase retention by up to 30 per cent.

This simple task activates the reticular activating system (RAS) in the brain, which is responsible for filtering out unnecessary information to help you focus on the goals that are important to you. The RAS also helps our brain absorb the desired outcome into our self-image imme-diately. Our brains have intricate reward and punishment mechanisms. With every achievement along the path to meeting our goals, our body releases dopamine into our brains, creating a sense of pleasure. This chemical mood elevation keeps us focused and motivated. We physically feel good when we're progressing towards a worthwhile goal.

By not reading your goals at these times, you're not putting the right programming into your brain. You will likely fail at your goals because you're not focusing on them, but also because other things will be programmed into your brain, such as negative media news, irrelevant social media or fiction. Failure to progress towards or meet a goal means the dopamine supply gets cut off and feelings of emptiness, sadness and inadequacy will replace the good feelings.

You can literally programme your mind like a computer and increase the supply of the addictive drug-like chemicals it produces to make you feel good.

A gift for you

At the start of *Life Leverage* I promised you some gifts. Here is the personal vision, values and goals document I use. It has space to fill in your vision, mission, values, KRAs and all types of goals (personal, family, how you want to be known, financial, material, career and business). I know that, if you use it, your life *will* change.

Here's my gift to you. Type the short link below into your browser, or, in the ebook, simply click on it. Thank you for getting this far and having faith in me to learn the Life Leverage philosophy:

http://goo.gl/2YstFU

- **Treat every day like the day before a holiday.**

Isn't it amazing how you can get a week's worth of work done the day before a holiday? How do you fit all of that in? Well, this is Parkinson's Law in effect. You could even call it Reverse Parkinson's Law, because instead of work expanding to fill the time available for its completion, time has contracted and you have filled it to the brim. If you lived every day as if it were the day before a two-week holiday, you would be productive, awesome and dangerous. Thank you, Brian Tracy, for teaching me this invaluable technique and mindset.

Other models and systems will be detailed in Chapter 22, 'Time models'.

Summary

All tasks are not equal, so you must prioritize and posteriorize to make sure that high-value tasks linked to your KRAs and IGTs are top of the list. If it gets you closer to your vision, it goes to the top of the list; if it doesn't, it goes to someone else, or in the bin. Simple. Keep checking your course against your vision. Remind yourself of your goals twice a day, before you go to bed and as soon as you wake up. This will make you feel great and it can increase retention by up to 30 per cent. Treat every day like it's the day before you go on holiday and you will be operating at optimum efficiency.

#20 Seasonal clear-out

Over time, stuff builds up and creates clutter. Clutter has been proven to be a distraction, and create bottlenecks, backlogs and time drains. According to unclutterer.com, researchers at the Princeton University Neuroscience Institute found that:

'Multiple stimuli present in the visual field at the same time compete for neural representation by mutually suppressing their evoked activity throughout the visual cortex, providing a neural correlate for the limited processing capacity of the visual system.'

To put that in non-neuroscience jargon, 'When your environment is cluttered, the chaos restricts your ability to focus. The clutter also limits your brain's ability to process information. Clutter makes you distracted and unable to process information as well as you do in an uncluttered, organized and serene environment.'

So it is for your email inbox, diary, files on your computer, office and physical personal space. Natural build-up will occur and catch up with you, just as a garage or basement will seem to fill itself with rubbish. Now we know why a good spring clean or seasonal clear-out feels so good! August and December are often good months to do these clear-outs as they are likely to have the least effect on your business (unless you hire out Santas) and mark the halfway and year-end points.

Here are the things you would benefit from clearing out:

- paper and office clutter – file it or fling it

- email inbox – do, delegate or delete

- diary – delete old recurrences and tasks and re-evaluate entries

- tasks and to-do lists – do, delegate or delete
- subscriptions – unsubscribe from all non-important sites
- belongings – get rid of possession clutter – sell or give to charity
- direct debits – check and cancel what you no longer use
- vision and values – check and tweak
- KRAs and goals – check and tweak.

Ask yourself, 'Am I still doing the right things to get me to my goals/vision? What can I get rid of that is a distraction?'

Summary

Decluttering your life improves brain function. Fact. Having a clear-out twice a year, when it will cause least disruption to your business, feels great and is progress towards your goal and vision. Clear out your office, inbox, diary, wardrobe, everything you can, to create a more serene environment in which to work and be more productive. You could even NeTime by listening to audio at the same time.

#21 Duplication disdain

One of the biggest time drains is duplication. Doing a task more than once to get a single outcome burns your life away and causes frustration. Have you ever written an important document or presentation and the computer has crashed or you lost the file? How good did that feel? Like you wanted to smash things?

Even worse than the cost of duplication is the compounded cost of duplication, either through the lasting knock-on opportunity cost of the time, or the fact that certain tasks could be duplicated many times over. One task that gets duplicated for just one hour, per week, will drain 2,080 hours over 40 years that you can never get back. If that time was worth just £50 per hour, that's a compounded loss of £104,000.

One of the most misunderstood clichéd phrases that comes out of business and personal development is 'It's OK to make a mistake; just never make the same mistake twice.' People don't make the same mistake twice; they usually make it 117 times until finally it gets bad enough and they are forced into change. If someone has anger management issues, they don't get angry once and then become Buddha. They probably get angry their whole life until something bad enough or important enough happens to almost force them to change it. My mum smoked for 40 years and was never going to give up, and then when Gemma became pregnant with our first child, Bobby Moore, she quit overnight. Wow. She had a bigger reason.

So the point is, people's habits play on repeat because that is how they are conditioned and that is who they are. Self-awareness, constant feedback and tweaking and an understanding (and total disdain) for duplication are vital.

The following cause duplication:

- lack of awareness and feedback
- lack of systems and centralization
- the wrong people
- lack of training and discipline
- lack of vision, planning and organization
- busyness, rushing, chaos, hard work.

Here they are in detail:

• Lack of awareness or feedback

If you are oblivious to what's being duplicated, it will carry on for ever. Continually ask yourself, your team and your customers, 'What should we start doing, stop doing and keep doing?' You'll soon remove duplication and wastage. And it will feel great!

• Lack of systems and centralization

Losing important emails, taking ages to find files on your computer, not having access to passwords, documents and remote drives when you need them, losing your notebook, repetition of tasks over and over, forgetting renewals and subscriptions … the list goes on and on.

One major solution to task duplication is systems and centralization. Centralizing your data, logins and passwords, files and documents all on the cloud with remote multi-device access will remove much of your daily duplication. Techies get excited about this because it increases efficiency, thereby reducing wastage and frustration.

Here are some of the simple systems you can implement immediately to avoid duplication and wastage:

- naming your files and emails logically for easy searching/filing/access

- one-page checklists for specific tasks

- reminders and diary entries for renewals, subscriptions and tasks

- centralized shareable to-do list accessible on all devices

- sharing of diary, email, document files

- automation (credit card pre-entry, auto login, etc.)

- single centralization – removing all duplicate files and so forth

- provision of manuals, video tutorials, audio files and recordings

- repurposing of products into multimedia.

The specific websites and apps for these systems are all detailed in the 'Mobile Lifestyle Blueprint' later in *Life Leverage*.

• The wrong people

Getting me to research and analyse is like expecting a cat to bark or your children to do what you tell them. A huge thanks to Suneep for the diligent research, data-mining and analysis for *Life Leverage*. It's a task I hate and am a disaster at, and one that he loves and is a master at.

As an entrepreneur, I used to think it highly leveraged to get team/staff members to do multiple tasks in their role. What nearly always happened was the things they hated and couldn't do caused a lot of pain for them in their role, stopped them enjoying the things they did love, and they ended up doing most things badly. You could have a great person in the wrong role or performing the wrong function, and they immediately become average or worse.

Be very clear on job descriptions for roles, instructions for tasks, and the right person to perform those functions. Be as clear on the type of person you want in the role as you are on the brief, project or job description. This will liberate many previously duplicated and wasted hours and maximize efficiency, leverage and satisfaction.

- **Lack of training and discipline**

To avoid duplication when training team members, think laterally and with leverage in mind, and then keep reiterating it until it becomes a habit. This is rarely done, but it's an absolute must-do. It is likely to be in your KRAs, and if it isn't perhaps it should be. Once effective and de-duplicated training is performed, then discipline is required to change the old habits to form the new, more efficient ones. Like learning to touch-type, at first it is hard and weird and slow and clunky. It actually takes longer than the two-index-finger method that most people use, you really want to revert back to your old ways to get the immediate task done more quickly. With a little practice and discipline each day you can easily type 65 words per minute. You have a new habit, you've removed wastage and duplication and you can leverage this for the rest of your life.

Training team members to remove duplication also involves them becoming decision-makers, self-reliant and motivated, and given access to systems, processes and answers they can find answers without having to go to you all the time. If there aren't the right processes or you use your power and ego to control them and make decisions for them, there will always be duplication of time between them and you.

- **Lack of vision, planning and organization**

According to Brian Tracy, ten to 12 minutes' planning saves 100 to 120 minutes in wasted time and diffused effort. And so it is for time duplication and wastage. Continually check and loop through your VVKIKs to ensure maximum Life Leverage and minimum time duplication. Just as planning an alternative route to avoid a traffic jam can save time and frustration, vision, planning and organization can save time for your tasks, KRAs and IGTs. Batch tasks together to avoid the wasted time between tasks, set your environment up so it's conducive for focused work, in isolation or inspiration, with everything one click away so you can get in flow and stay in flow for the optimum amount of time.

- **Busyness, rushing, chaos, hard work**

Running around like a headless chicken is the antithesis of vision, planning and organization. We convince and delude ourselves that cracking on with it and working hard are the right way, yet we could be going harder the wrong way.

Rushing always creates more work, mistakes and having to do the task again, properly. Chaos makes it impossible to find anything you've done before or need now.

Never be too busy to be strategic. Most people complain that they don't have time to plan and be strategic but ten to 12 minutes can do it, according to Brian Tracy.

Summary

Duplication of tasks is frustrating and time-consuming and ultimately costs you money. Get rid of duplication by doing the following: be aware of where the duplications are, centralize your data, logins and so on, get the right people to do the right tasks and train yourself and your team to do things more efficiently using the right processes. Stop running around like a headless chicken and take some time to plan and be strategic. It only takes ten to 12 minutes to get focused so you can stay in-flow for longer.

illustration, vision, planning and organization can save time for your tasks, KRAs and JDTs. Batch tasks together to avoid the wasted time between tasks. Set your environment up so it is conducive for focused work, in isolation or in conjunction with everything one click away so you can get in flow and stay in flow for the optimum amount of time.

Busyness, rushing, chaos, hard work

Running around like a headless chicken is the antithesis of vision, planning and organization. We convince and delude ourselves that cracking on with it and working hard are the right way, yet we could be going harder the wrong way.

Rushing always creates more work, mistakes and having to do the task again, properly. Chaos makes it impossible to find anything you've done before or need now.

Never be too busy to be strategic. Most people complain that they don't have time to plan and be strategic but ten to 12 minutes can do it, according to Brian Tracy.

Summary

Making most of tasks, KRAs, JDTs and time is crucial and ultimately decides your 'money stream' of domination system. The following are ways of making the most as they come up, often alongside catchpoints. Carry on, perfect the process, serve the people, serve the system, that works, spread and scale it in 10x lots, more efficiently using 1 per task. Finally, stop running around like a headless chicken; ten to 12 minutes time to plan and be strategic a day can save you 12 minutes to deliberation process and can save you now for money.

#22 Time models

This chapter is about systemizing your time (life) management with easy-to-use tools and models that follow the Life Leverage philosophy. Forget old regurgitated corporate spiel or gimmicky tools that work for five minutes but are hard or boring to maintain; these models and systems honour and understand time and make it easier to master your time, and therefore your life.

TIME INVESTED, SPENT AND WASTED (TI, TS, TW)

- **Ti** – Time invested
- **Ts** – Time spent
- **Tw** – Time wasted

In reverse order of importance:

- **Tw – Time wasted**

Anything that is a time-drain-suck is time wasted. Have you ever said to yourself 'Well, I'll never get that time back?' Sure you have. We all have. The challenge is that it is so easy to get sucked into Tw. Things that drain time have already been listed and it's not worth wasting any more time on them. Cut them out completely, like carbs or MSG.

- **Ts – Time spent**

Time spent is time that can have low or high value in financial or emotional terms, but it has no residual benefit. Working for an hourly rate, doing a task, or exchanging your time for money, is time spent. You can never get it back, and neither can you get any ongoing recurring value or benefit from it. Unsuccessful people 'spend' most, if not all, of their time. Low-value hourly rates and salaries fall under Ts. Even good salaries fall into the Ts category. Much of the work you're doing, imposed upon you by others but not high on your values or leading you towards your vision, falls under Ts.

- ## Ti – Time invested

Time invested continues to earn or give leverage long after that task was completed. Ti has residual and recurring benefit. Buying a property is Ti; building your team and training them is Ti. New knowledge that gets you better results is Ti that you can leverage for the rest of your life. Ti has a passive, recurring benefit long after the time is spent. Ironically and paradoxically, in business and life, many of the highest-value Ti tasks don't pay immediately, but they do pay for a long time into the future, maybe even for ever.

Leveraging, leading, inspiring, influencing, managing, outsourcing, networking, training and building systems, educating yourself, time with mentors and in masterminds, are all examples of time invested (Ti).

Become aware of where you are spending all of your time in one of the three areas above. Waste no time, spend less time, and invest more time. Passive income comes from time invested. Dividends come from time invested. Salaries come from time spent. There's nothing wrong with exchanging time for money, as long as there is a vision to invest it. You can work hard for your money or you can make your money work hard for you.

Measure and monitor your time to master it. Be strict, ruthless and disciplined with where you invest it. Lead, manage and leverage. It's not about how much you do, but how much the world is doing for you and for your vision. Then you preserve time to have more to do the things you love, things that build you a future, things that make you money.

You can choose that you are only going to do what you love, what you want, and what makes you money, and the rest can be delegated or leveraged, and you can let all that serve your vision. That's often the best choice anyway because many of those things that you don't love you're probably not the best at anyway. One of the most liberating things in the world is to do more of what you love and are great at, the things that serves your vision, and to outsource or leverage all the things you hate or turn into a car crash. That is real freedom. And the person who does the outsourced task for you probably loves it and is certainly better at it than you are. This frees you up to serve more people.

RETURN ON TIME INVESTED (RoTI)

Return on time invested (RoTI) is a model and modus operandi in one. It is a system to follow to analyse how you are using your time, and it is a Life Leverage philosophy, a way of thinking.

Consistently ask yourself: 'Will this give me the best return on time invested?'

This simple question will force you to keep checking that you are using your time well, performing the right tasks and also getting maximum leverage. It will force you to earn the maximum amount of money in the minimum amount of time, and create the most recurring, residual and passive benefit on every function.

TIME OPPORTUNITY COST (TOC)

Time opportunity cost (TOC) is the cost of the current task or time spent. Most people don't know what this is or can't see it, because all they can see is the benefit or drawback of what they are doing, and not the benefit or drawback of what they aren't doing or could be doing instead.

In financial terms, opportunity cost is simple to measure. If, for example, you have cash in the bank and interest rates are net 1 per cent compared to a net return of 5 per cent on a property, then the opportunity cost is net 4 per cent if you leave the money in the bank. You get 1 per cent interest in the bank, but it cost you 4 per cent by not having your money in the property.

Time is less measurable to many, but the concept is the same. It's not just what you are doing that is costing you money, it is what you aren't doing. It's also not just what you are doing that is making you money, it's what you are not doing. Like RoTI, keep monitoring and measuring two things: how you are investing your time, and what you are not doing with your time.

DO, DELEGATE, DEFER OR DELETE (THE 4Ds)

Do, delegate, defer or delete (the 4Ds) is a four-step system and Life Leverage guide to the choices you have for any task. It is so simple, with only four choices, so it helps with overwhelm, confusion and frustration. Follow the 4D system for any task to become more efficient, effective and decisive. See Chapter 22 for more on this.

TO-DO AND NOT-TO-DO LISTS

While writing things down has proven and valuable benefits, to-do lists can get as overwhelming as the tasks themselves. Here's how most people run to-do lists. (Of course, you've never done this!)

1. You brain-dump all the tasks that need to be done.

2. There are too many things to do and you don't know where to even start.

3. You know you should order them in priority, so you do.

4. You know you should do the most important, urgent, high-IGT task, but you can see an 'easy-quick-win' task at No.7, so you do that instead.

5. You check your email, Facebook page, take a little break, answer the phone.

6. You get back to the to-do list an hour later, and you know you've got to do No.1 but you really want to make the to-do list look smaller, so you start with No.5.

7. No.5 gets hard so you stop part of the way through and look for an easy one. No.9 won't take long.

8. You just remembered something you did yesterday, so you write it on your list and immediately cross it out. Progress!

9. You experiment with boxes, letters and numbers of priority and to-do list apps, convinced that they will make the tasks easier.

10. Nagging at you are No.1 and No.2, which are really important and getting more urgent and overwhelming all the time.

And so it goes round and round and round. You keep looking for the next gimmick – like using a fitness app that will make you lose weight more easily. But nothing changes.

So here are some sustainable systems for to-do lists:

1. Eat that frog!

2. How do you eat an elephant?

3. The five-to-seven rule

4. Not-to-do list

5. To-leverage list

6. L1, M2, DL

7. IGT and IGV.

Let's look at each of these in turn:

1. Eat that frog!

Suck it up and do the most important thing first, and early. Isolate yourself and get stuck in. No excuses: just do it *right now*. Do the hardest thing first and the rest of the day will be easy. Do the most urgent or most important thing before everyone else gets out of bed and you will increase your self-worth as well as your results. The more you do this, the more endorphins you'll trigger in your brain, and the more you will anchor and train yourself to do it.

2. How do you eat an elephant?

One bite at a time. So what if the task is writing a book, running a marathon or building an empire? All you can do is the broken-down, smaller task that is right in front of you, right now. Set the big goal, then focus on the small task to stop yourself from being overwhelmed by the behemoth goal you've set or project you've got with a looming deadline.

3. The five-to-seven rule

Put five to seven things on your to-do list, *only*. No more than seven. No. 8 is not urgent, so don't even write it down. You can write all your tasks down, dump them out of your brain, and then above them take out and list the five to seven that you need to do. Now you have something achievable in front of you and you can get stuck in.

4. Not-to-do list

If you have your five to seven most important tasks written above your full list of brain-dumped tasks, then in between the two write your not-to-dos.

DO NOT:

1. Check email.

2. Check Facebook.

3. Answer the phone.

4. Go and look in the fridge.

5. Google anything.

6. Put the TV on.

5. To-leverage list

If your to-do list is called a to-do list, then your brain will pick up on the 'doing'. You are subconsciously asking your brain to do something. If you rename your to-do list your 'to-leverage' list, then you are programming your brain to perform leverage rather than action.

6. L1, M2, DL

A new system for your new 'to-leverage' list is L1, M2, DL:

- Leverage first.

- Manage second.

- Do last!

When you're busy, perhaps the first thing you think is 'What do I need to do? or 'I've got so much to do, where do I even start?' or 'When can I get this done?' or 'How can I do this?'

Now try this: next time you start your task or to-do list, instead of starting with a task, start with what you can leverage or outsource. Who can you get to do the first task you were going to do?

And the second. And the third. Out of seven tasks for the day, if you've leveraged four of them and you do three of them, you'll achieve more than double the results in less than half the time.

But, unfortunately, once you've leveraged out tasks you would ordinarily have done yourself, they don't just magically arrive on your desk the next day in shiny wrapping paper. Any task 'leveraged' needs managing through to completion. Check through your leveraged tasks and manage (guide) them through to completion. Only once you have gone through these two steps should you even consider 'doing' a task. A few small hours moved from 'doing' to 'leveraging', from time spent (Ts) to time invested (Ti) has huge compounded benefits. You might end up leveraging three tasks, having two 'under management (being managed)' and only two that you actually have to do.

And, if you're too busy to invest time, that's probably the very reason you need to do it. And if no one can do that task or job as well as you, that's probably the very reason you need to do it, too.

7. IGT and IGV

The only way to know for sure whether you are leveraging correctly, whether the tasks you are doing are of the highest financial value to you, and whether the tasks you're outsourcing are beneath your financial value, is to know what you're worth, per hour of your time.

The first stage is to calculate your Income-Generating Value (IGV). Your IGV is what you are worth, per hour of work. When you know exactly what an hour of your time is worth, you can calculate accurately what tasks you should do yourself and what tasks you should leverage out, pay for, or inspire others to do for you.

To calculate your IGV, add up the total number of hours you spend working every week. That includes your job/career, any part-time work, and any time you're putting into property or asset building – the entire amount of time attributed to earning money. You might have something like 55 hours.

Now calculate, or roughly guess, how much money you earn in that time frame. Include all sources of gross income: salary, dividend, interest, property income if you have it, and so on. Include all income not including gifts or loans, and add up the gross amount (not net of taxes etc.). You may have £850 in a week. If you know what you earn per month, not per week, divide your monthly figure by 4.3 to get your weekly figure. Now divide the amount of gross income by the total amount of work hours, and you have your IGV – your time value per hour. Every hour you work brings in, on average, £x.

In this example: *IGV = £850 / 55 hours = £15.46 per hour*

Or: *IGV = total income (week) / hours worked (week)*

So what does this tell you? Every task that will (or could) bring in more than £15.46, it's OK to do yourself. This could be a 'do' task on your 'to-leverage' list. You could do this task yourself without diminishing your IGV. But every task that brings in (or could bring in) less than £15.46 per hour, or you could pay £15.45 or less to outsource, must be outsourced. If you don't, your IGV will go down.

This compounds, because when you free time from lower-value tasks to higher-value tasks, you bring in more money and it compounds back into the IGV.

This is why people don't get rich by working longer employed hours or doing overtime. This is why the rich get richer: it's because they leverage, outsource and pay for the lower-value tasks.

In order for this to work for you, you need to be disciplined with yourself, and have faith in this 'model'. Any task that comes your way that you feel will, or could, earn you more than your IGV, then do it yourself, because it will pay you to do it. If you keep doing that, your IGV will go up and up and up.

But even more importantly, every task that comes your way that will or could bring in less than your IGV, you must leverage or outsource. Either blag a favour, do a reciprocal deal, or pay for the task to be done via one of the outsourcing websites mentioned in the next section, or a local virtual assistant. Or your mum/dad. Or your children. If you don't, you'll get poorer and you'll actually repel more money than you pull in. Stick to this system and it will change your life and finances for ever.

80/20 IGV

Your IGV calculation isn't the full story. If we add the 80/20 Principle and the Life Leverage philosophy to your IGV, it looks very different. If we add the 80/20 Principle to your earning capacity or IGV, then it stands to reason that 80 per cent of your IGV comes from 20 per cent of the things you do, and conversely 20 per cent of your IGV comes from 80 per cent of the things you do.

Here's how it affects your IGV:

1. 80 per cent of your income comes from 20 per cent of your work time.

2. 20 per cent of your income comes from 80 per cent of your work time.

Let's take a look at what this means:

1. 20 per cent of the things you do bring in 80 per cent of your income.

This means that you earn four times your IGV in a fifth of the time you work. You could literally drop four-fifths of your work time and only earn 20 per cent less than working your full week. If you just reversed a fifth of your time, you'd earn more in two-fifths of your time using 80/20 than you did doing a full working week not using the 80/20 Principle.

2. 80 per cent of the things you do bring in 20 per cent of your income.

This means that you earn just a fifth of your money in 80 per cent of the time you work. You are spending four-fifths of your time earning just one-fifth of your total income. This is draining your life and giving you hardly any financial benefit. Imagine if you could reverse this 80 per cent time and turn it into high-IGV 20 per cent time ...

The difference between high-IGV 20 per cent time and low-IGV 80 per cent time is extreme. Your high-IGV 20 per cent time earns you 16 times more money than your low 80 per cent IGV. If you want to calculate your 20 per cent and 80 per cent IGV, the calculations are:

20/80 IGV = total income (week) x 80% / hours worked (week) x 20%

80/20 IGV = total income (week) x 20% / hours worked (week) x 80%

You will never see things the same way again now that you know this!

Exercise: Keep a work log

For the next two weeks, create a simple work log of how you are spending your work time (career, business, part-time income opportunities and any other 'work'). Have a Word document open, or a sheet of paper or notes folder on your smartphone. Every hour that you work in a day, note briefly what you did. Be honest with yourself, including all wasted time or distracted tasks, and at the end of the day put the letters IGT next to the parts that were income generating.

At the end of the two weeks, work out what percentage of your time, is spent on IGTs. If you're anything like me, you'll probably be shocked at how just a few hours bring in most of the money and results, and a huge amount of time is virtually wasted, with little or no financial benefit. Once you know where you are spending your time, you can implement 20/80 leverage for maximum financial gain with minimal effort and wastage, by doing only the highest IGTs and outsourcing or dropping the rest.

When you use these proven models and systems for time and life management, all other parts of your life, especially your free time and earning capacity, will dramatically improve.

Fair warning, there's a price to pay. That price is discipline. However, if you have a clear vision and are living out your values, then you need no motivation or discipline to do those things of highest value to you.

These exact time models have enabled me to build seven different business/income streams of more than seven figures a year, each. Today I don't work at all because business, property, personal development, money and finance, teaching and writing are all passions of mine. I'm in the office no more than a couple of hours a day, and the office runs itself 99 per cent of the time. I play golf with Bobby every day, and spend hours a day with my fiancée and daughter. We spend three to four months a year in Grand Cayman, Monaco, Florida and Dubai so that Bobby can compete in world golf championships. This is all financed by passive income from assets. Freedom is one of my higher values and these models and systems have given me this freedom for which I'm humbly grateful. It's a good job because I've become completely unemployable now – always thinking about leverage and with a big authority complex, I'd get fired in minutes, just like Bob did in the story I told you at the beginning of the book!

Despite all of this, I'm the most unlikely person to have created this leveraged, ideal mobile lifestyle because I always believed in hard work and was raised by a strong father who believed the same, and forged his livelihood with brute force and long hours. I worked hard at school and got good grades, worked hard running my family pub and even harder as an artist, yet made virtually no money in these ventures. I had no free time and was barely ever above the financial breadline. It was the societal conditioning, lack of both education and a team, and zero understanding of the Life Leverage philosophy that held me back. As you will discover in Section 4, there is another way, and it's a simple system that you can follow, too.

Summary

There are several models that make it easier to master your time, and therefore your life. Rather than wasting time, spend time on high-value tasks, or outsource the tasks and invest your time in things that have residual and recurring benefit, like property or building assets. Monitor and measure your time. Keep a work log. Have no more than seven items on your to-do list. Do, delegate, defer or delete, eat that frog, and that elephant, one bite at a time, make sure not to do anything that is distracting or a waste of time. Leverage, leverage, leverage. Remember that 20 per cent of the things you do bring in 80 per cent of the income. Working out which 20 per cent of your IGTs this is will reduce wastage and increase your financial gain.

Section 4: Blueprint

This section gives you the operations you need for outsourcing everything and creating a mobile lifestyle. Creating your ideal mobile life is about the mindset, skillset and operations of elimination, automation and liberation. This includes the way you think and function, and the sites, apps and devices you choose and use to give you global mobility and lifestyle.

Warning: this section is the antithesis of how society has indoctrinated you. Much of what you are about to learn is known only by an elite few who have questioned normality and convention enough to learn a better way, despite the short-term challenges.

If you had been with me around the mastermind table in Grand Cayman in February 2015, you'd have seen the biggest and final aha-lightbulb epiphany I have ever experienced in creating a fully leveraged, mobile lifestyle. And it was a complete U-turn on what had previously brought me success. You see, we were discussing ways to create a fully mobile life. Everyone was grateful and loving the Cayman experience – you could get so used to spending a few months a year in the places you love, with the people you love, not having to work hard for a living. I was listing the apps and tools I'd used that give time and location freedom, and Dave, one of the mentors and a multi-millionaire too, interrupted me and said, 'Rob, do you still have an office in the office?' Slightly confused, I answered, 'Er, yes, of course.' Dave replied, 'Well, you're not fully mobile then yet, are you?'

As soon as I landed back in the UK, I organized the demolition of the wall that separated my office from the main open-plan office and filled it with five staff members. I installed boardroom facilities in my dining room at home (hands-free connectivity to a large screen for presentations, a larger boardroom table, etc.), and got remote access to the work central server that I previously needed to go to the office to access.

While I felt freedom because I owned the business, and financially could be funded as I travelled around the globe, I was actually still attached to a location and therefore not fully mobile. Dave, who owns businesses in three continents, had sold shares in his business and moved to Grand Cayman. Still being paid handsomely by his business and not needed for the day-to-day running of it, he saw the final piece in the puzzle for me, and his advice helped me get the last 5 per cent complete that makes 95 per cent of the difference in creating a mobile lifestyle.

To be honest, I was going back into the office each day not because I was needed but more because I was emotionally attached to it. Yes, I was systemically attached to the server, but I enjoyed the buzz and autonomy, still wanted to watch over it, and more often than not all I did was get in everyone's way so as to keep myself feeling important and valued.

This section will take you on the same journey to set up systems for a fully mobile life, and deal with the surprising mindset and emotional barriers that can get in the way of freedom, authority and full Life Leverage.

#23 The Mobile Lifestyle Blueprint

The Mobile Lifestyle Blueprint (MLB) on the next page is the complete plan and system for outsourcing everything and creating a mobile life. The MLB's central theme is freedom, with three overriding principles, three main mindsets and three main systems for full Life Leverage.

The three overriding principles of full freedom are:

- scale and solution

- leverage

- passion–profession merge.

The three mindsets are:

- automation (via systems)

- letting go (to the team/network)

- service vision (wealth and legacy).

The three systems are:

- mobile systems

- network (team)

- wealth (legacy).

Below we look at each concept in more detail.

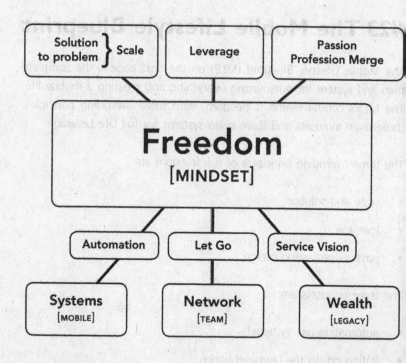

- calendar
- email
- cloud-based file sharing
- social media
- customer relationship management
- banking
- e-commerce
- audiobooks
- office drive

- password protection
- remote AV
- managing director
- operations manager
- PA/VA
- specialists
- financiers

- cash flow
- capital
- net worth
- physical assets
- passive

FREEDOM

The central theme of the MLB is freedom. Freedom is both a mindset and skillset; a Life Leverage philosophy and set of systems.

You can have all the systems in the world, but freedom ultimately comes from the mind, as proven by Viktor Frankl and his experiences in the Nazi concentration camps, mentioned in Chapter 11. Conversely, you can be free in the mind, controlling your thoughts and feelings, but be tied to an office, a boss or a geographic location. The secret is to deal with and merge both in equal measure, which is exactly what the MLB does.

A freedom mindset, central to the MLB, takes full responsibility for thoughts, feelings and actions. No matter how well you systemize and automate your enterprise, you will always get the odd surprise. Systems will break. People will mess up. New challenges will emerge when old ones are solved. You can never have true freedom from systems alone; you have to be able to control your thoughts and feelings to feel free, even when you get sucked back into operations.

The single best way to experience freedom is through gratitude. The gratitude mindset appreciates everything you have, whether you are on the way, in the way or just starting the way. You are grateful for the time-saving and liberating systems you create, and also for the challenges they give you setting them up and getting them automated. Pinning all your happiness on the completion and automation of every single system delays happiness and causes that feeling of 'never enough'. It also creates extreme frustration and self-worth issues when things temporarily break and need solving.

THE THREE MLB PRINCIPLES

Here are the three overriding principles of full freedom detailed:

1. Scale and solution

Much of the detail of 'Scale and solution' has been covered in 'Serving and solving', in Chapter 12. Your results, finance and freedom are directly relative to and a consequence of the problems you solve. Your mindset and ability to solve problems, in your own business and for others, give freedom because you don't let problems break you mentally, and you get the issues systematically fixed as quickly as possible. Just the very fact that you have focus on solving problems reduces the amount of problems you experience. You will never eradicate all problems, so your ability to accept that and still feel freedom, and then work to solve them by improving your systems, is what actually creates freedom.

You can't run away from responsibility, staff, customers or a service mentality. I've met many people lured into the 'laptop lifestyle', deluded by the fantasy of no staff, no customers, no dealing with people, no overheads, no responsibility – just a laptop and a money-counting machine. Such people are naive and misguided. The more that you want for your life, the more you rely on the scale of your enterprise, including number of staff, customers, processes, fixed costs and general responsibilities. Trying to get rid of them is counter-intuitive, but having the mindset of freedom and service is the solution, and the paradox is that trying to remove them creates less freedom and embracing more of them is the answer.

Not everyone wants vast scale, and that's OK. You don't have to be the next Steve Jobs visionary or have the responsibilty of 2 million employees like Walmart. You might not want thousands of employees, tens of millions in fixed costs, or millions of people having an opinion of you, but the size of your own vision will require a scale to match it.

2. Leverage

The entire Life Leverage philosophy merges into this part of the MLB: the leverage mindset, hiring, outsourcing, KRAs and IGTs, 80/20 thinking, time-saving models and systems, vision, leadership and management, getting more done in less of your personal time and letting go, so you can grow.

3. Passion–profession merge

When your vocation is your vacation and your passion your profession, you have freedom. No work to run away from and home to yearn for, just all and everything merged into one inspired life.

THE THREE MLB MINDSETS

Here are the three overriding mindsets of the Mobile Lifestyle Blueprint:

1. Automation (via systems)

The automation mindset and skillset is about making yourself redundant, not reliant. Through systems, apps and processes you remove reliance on you, bottlenecks and dependency, creating autonomy, automation and liberation. Automation disdains duplication, wastage and over-reliance on general people, skilled technicians and memory retention. Automation is striving for the shortest, simplest and easiest way to maximum productivity and efficiency, achieving maximum leverage.

Implementing the following systems will give you automation, global mobility and therefore freedom:

- calendar/diary

- email

- cloud-based file sharing

- social

- customer relationship management

- banking

- e-commerce
- audiobooks and ebooks
- office drive/server
- password protection
- remote AV.

Here are the relevant details and specifics required to get you operationally automated:

- **Calendar/diary**

Use a cloud-hosted calendar/diary system like Outlook, iCal or Google calendar. Don't use a quirky or little-known calendar as there will be bugs and synchronizing them with other users will be hard. You will need your calendar synchronized and accessible on every device you use (tablet, laptop, home PC, workstation), and accessible by the relevant people (PA, MD, relevant staff, husband, wife, etc.). This needs to be easy to use so that compartmentalizing your time, managing your appointments and blocking out time drains can be supported by everyone without confusion, duplication or time wastage.

I'm very non-technical. I don't enjoy setting up systems and if it's not on the first page of Google then it doesn't exist. So if I can do this, you can do this too. If you enjoy setting up these systems and playing with your devices, then great; if not, get your 13-year-old child to do it, or someone you know who is good with computers. Outsource the setting up of this and you get NeTime leverage.

- **Email**

As this is one of the biggest time drains, mastering email is very important. Centralize all email accounts across all devices, and make them easy to access. Maintain the ability to access them separately, and all together in one place, without having to open new browsers, log in, log out and mess about. You can give your PA access to your email to manage the wastage for you.

Follow this Life Leverage email management system for hyper-productivity and ruthless efficiency. You can literally receive hundreds of emails a day and stay on top, keep your inbox empty and maintain your time freedom.

Set up the following folders in your email host (Gmail, Outlook, etc.):

* General email
* Immediate response
* Awaiting (urgent) reply
* Business/promotion.

People use their inbox way too much. Having too many emails in their inbox makes them feel sick just looking at them. Instant overwhelm. They try to use the search facility in their inbox and often can't find anything. They never feel on top of things. Of course, this isn't you!

So your goal should be to keep your inbox EMPTY.

Every email that comes in should be dealt with using the 4D system: Do, Delegate, Defer or Delete.

* **Do:** A quick, easy win to do, or urgent or highly important.
* **Delegate**: Instruct someone else to do it.

- **Defer:** Important to do, but not right now.

- **Delete:** Delete immediately.

Here's what you do with each:

Do: Either reply/send right away (and then FILE or DELETE the email) or file into IMMEDIATE RESPONSE.

Delegate: Instruct someone else to do it but COPY YOURSELF in and file the copy into AWAITING (URGENT) REPLY.

Defer: File in GENERAL EMAIL or IMMEDIATE RESPONSE.

Delete: Smoke. For ever. I dare you!

So, an email comes in. If it's not important, put it in GENERAL EMAIL, a folder for general things. Check this folder two to three times a week only. Follow up on what you feel like following up on, let everything go or let the email stay until you need it later, and can search in this file.

If it's important/urgent, either (a) do it right now and then file the email, or (b) move to IMMEDIATE RESPONSE (IR). Follow up on IR at least twice per day, in focused time away from distractions (in isolation), but not in a reactive fashion as they come in. You control when you follow up to IR.

Your email in IR will either be Do or Delegate, so Do or Delegate. Copy yourself in on the action you take so you have a filed record (and therefore you don't have to search that massive 'Sent' folder). If you DELEGATE, copy yourself in, (a) because people think it's more important and (b) you will file this email in AWAITING (Urgent) REPLY.

- Awaiting (urgent) reply is for delegated tasks you need to manage, measure or follow up on. Check this folder once a day to check and chase all delegated tasks. Once it's done, delete or file the email.

- Business/promotion: you can file all business, marketing, subscriptions, promotions you get in this folder. You could also file this in general email, but people like to separate the two. Read this in breaks, free time, NeTime, when you have nothing to do, etc. Of course, if this is urgent or important, it goes into IR – like any Progressive or Rob Moore emails you might subscribe to.

• Cloud-hosted file sharing

Use a cloud-hosted file-sharing platform to save and share files that need to be shared or accessed remotely. Dropbox or WeTransfer are the most universal and are easy to use. You can be anywhere in the world and share and access files, presentations, video and audio of large file sizes without having to be geographically restricted.

• Social media

Have all your social platform apps you use regularly, such as Facebook, Twitter, Instagram, LinkedIn, WhatsApp, all downloaded, installed and the password entered on all your devices. Ease and mobility of access centrally means that you can comment, share and perform marketing tasks in real time. Be careful not to let them drain your time or become a social junkie.

• Customer relationship management

If you run a business or do any online marketing, remote access to your CRM (customer relationship management) and email-marketing databases are essential. Most services now host all data on the cloud, so remote access should be easy. You can make sales and business calls and send email messages and marketing from anywhere in the world.

- **Banking**

Most major banks now have advanced apps from which you can fully manage your accounts. A bit of time to set up security, payee details and synchronizing online memberships means that you can pay, move and receive money from anywhere in the world, between your accounts or to and from other people or companies. Because of e-signatures now, you can even exchange and complete on buying houses remotely.

Previously, paying money in, out and around has been a major faff and has restricted freedom. Not any more. You can have all your business accounts on one user interface. All your property accounts, partnerships, joint-venture accounts, current and savings accounts are all one tap or fingerprint away. If you exceed limits in savings where your cash is guaranteed by the bank, you can just set up another account with another bank.

- **E-commerce**

You can use online merchants such as PayPal and Worldpay from your apps too, just like the bank accounts. You can have business merchants so you can accept payments online anywhere in the world. You can even use companies like iZettle that will give you an app or a machine that can take money from credit and debit cards. Your business is now global.

- **Audiobooks and ebooks**

Audiobooks and ebooks allow you to learn from anywhere in the world without having to carry your library around with you. Kindle, iTunes and Audible make the ability to buy information easier and can store it on the cloud for you. You can access thousands of books from your device, ready to instantly consume when travelling, in the gym, stuck in a queue or traffic jam, while shopping alone; any time, anyplace, anywhere.

You can also use audio recording software instead of traditional pen and paper, and then have the audio transcribed for tasks and outsourcing instructions. You can use these audio recordings to create operations manuals for your business, and have a VA/outsourcer create and compile the information for you. There are text-reading apps that enable you to copy text from an image into a document, and screen recording apps that enable you to record a screen and voice for a sales presentation (gotowebinar.com), a conference meeting (gotomeeting.com) or for training purposes (camtasia.com). You can perform all of these anywhere in the world from your app or device.

• Office drive/server

The final piece in the puzzle of a global, fully mobile lifestyle for me was knocking down the walls of my office and giving the space to my staff. The only two things at that time that were keeping me tied to the office, albeit for only a couple hours a day, were my need for importance and access to all the office files through the local office server. Through LogMeIn.com or remote connection, you can now access local drives internationally; all you need is a password and Wi-Fi. You could even spy on local computers and through internal cameras remotely, if you are really paranoid!

• Password protection

There's little more annoying than having to put your passwords into every website and payment gateway. You know you need good passwords that are hard to hack, but the more you have the fewer you remember. There are two solutions. Download a master password and hidden notes app. The one I use is mSecure, and you can keep all passwords, sensitive data, important numbers like National Insurance number, passport, mortgage account numbers, other passwords, pins, login details, your net-worth statement, and any other secrets you have. This way you have access to absolutely everything from an app on your phone, anywhere in the world.

The second solution is to use auto-login software or browser plug-in. Any non-sensitive sites and logins can be auto-logged in. Just don't use these for payment-related sites, and ensure that your master password is not the same as any other password you use; it should be unique, memorable to you and hard to hack.

- **Remote AV**

When you create your ideal mobile lifestyle, it's likely, though not oblig-atory, that you will travel more. You'll do more of what you want, when you want, with whom you want. The more you travel, the more you need to manage your security at home. Through apps and services like Control4, you can fully automate your home. You can set up CCTV at home, inside and out, and access it from your phone or device while you are in another country. You can turn your lights and TV and music on and off from the other side of the world, or predetermine a time to do so to mimic living patterns. You can control the heating, access and control the door locking, and even go as far as opening and closing the curtains.

While at first I set some of this up out of a love for boy's toys, it has become a valuable part of a fully mobile lifestyle. You can add things piece by piece to your system, starting with music and TV, and adding full security as your net worth and travel time increase.

2. Letting go (to the team/network)

Building a team and leveraging a skilled network is one of the most important principles and shortcuts to living the Life Leverage philosophy. Go back through Chapter 16, 'Letting go and saying "No"', to remind yourself of the attributes of building and leveraging your mastermind network.

Your network will have a direct impact on your net worth. It is said that you are the sum of the five people you spend the most time with: you become the sixth. Observe the people you spend the most time with and be strategic in whom you need to add and drop from your network. Change your peer group if necessary, and look to be the least experienced or least wealthy person in your network/circles and you will get dragged up to their level much faster than with people at or below your level who are likely to hold you back.

We all know when starting out in business that it can be lonely or challenging without support or guidance. The upside of your ready-made network is the virtually leveraged building of your business and personal operations, because everything that you need, and that would take an age to find yourself, is on tap through your leveraged network. Building your network and developing the key partnerships and relationships should always be a top-priority KRA and IGT.

The key team members for maximum results with minimum time wastage are:

- PA/VA
- operations manager
- managing director
- specialists/technicians
- financiers.

Let's look at each one in turn.

- **PA/VA**

Your personal assistant (or virtual assistant) is the first person you want in your team, as quickly as possible, probably before you think you need them, to help you scale towards your vision. If there's one most common mistake entrepreneurs make, it is working too hard *in* the business rather than *on* the business. I'm yet to meet a fellow entrepreneur who didn't get in their own way at some point and slow their own growth. Looking back, almost every successful person I've talked to or interviewed, felt that they should have hired or got help sooner.

It might have been harder in the Industrial Age, when staff costs and overheads were higher and more location-specific. But in today's Technology Age, you can use outsourcing websites like elance.com, peopleperhour.com, fiverr.com, rent-acoder.com, freelancer.co.uk, guru. com and many more to hire people globally, by the month, week, day, hour or even by the minute. You can literally build your team with zero contract, minimum investment, by job or task, from your laptop anywhere in the world. You aren't responsible for their health and safety or taking on high wages or overheads, and you can pay as you go. There is virtually no risk.

Before you think you are ready, which is right now, log on to all of these outsourcing sites, set up a profile (or, better, get someone to do it for you) and start hiring outsourcers for small jobs as a start and test. Give easy jobs, or jobs you hate, but which won't take too long. These can include transcribing, slide presentations on Keynote or PowerPoint, research, finding apps, buying your books and products online, booking travel, tickets and venues, setting up your IT and systems (see above), buying gifts, managing other outsourcers, cleaners, gardeners, etc., buying and selling on eBay, website design, branding, arranging couriers ... the list goes on.

Many of these functions can be outsourced quickly, easily and cost-effectively. The key to speed and size of scale is to start them now, even before you really need them, even if you can do it yourself quickly and easily, because you are testing the different outsourcers, people, websites and platforms to find the best ones for you to work with, and preparing to have an established relationship by the time the big and important functions need leveraging. When it comes to really needing help and leverage, you will be very busy and overwhelmed and it will be harder and take longer. If you think ahead and have a little vision, you will move seamlessly from a few little sideline tasks to having multiple specialist VAs running vital parts of your business the Life Leverage way, preserving your time and allowing you to focus on high-value KRAs and IGTs.

You should aim as fast as possible to get a real PA, local to you, who manages all your affairs. If you've watched *Suits*, you need your very own Donna. I believe a great PA is one of the very best investments you can make, will pay their wages many times over and free you to scale and serve. Richard Branson reputedly has five PAs. I have two and I can honestly say I think I would short-circuit without the great help and support I get from them.

The first person we recruited at Progressive was my business partner Mark's mum, Catherine. VAs weren't as well known or easy to access back in 2006. Mark's mum helped us because she loved her son; it was a cost-effective way for us to leverage! We leveraged her time and her love for Mark. She worked at Progressive for six years before fully and finally retiring.

The second person we recruited at Progressive was *my* mum. She still works with us too, ten years on and counting, and she loves it. And I get to see a lot more of my mum than I used to, which is one of the greatest gifts the Life Leverage philosophy can bring. We hired estate agents to buy for us and paid low basic salaries and very high commissions, we offered properties for design work and IT services and a host of other 'contra' deals – we did what we had to do to get leverage, even when we didn't have much spare cash to pay people. The hardest part, like the 80 per cent of the fuel being needed to get a Space Shuttle off the ground, was getting our first couple of people, the first small steps. After that, you think nothing of growing and scaling and hiring more of the best people.

But, looking back, we were far slower than we should have been. You don't have to be, because you can leverage my experience and mistakes for faster results. We managed to get people working for Progressive's vision because they felt part of it. That was more important than the money, and still is today for many of the team. Use the power of your vision to leverage the gap between no staff and a full mastermind power team.

- **Operations manager**

Your operations manager manages the day-to-day operations of your enterprise. Because most entrepreneurs make poor managers and don't like it anyway, this is a key position to fill as quickly as possible. The sooner you can remove yourself from day-to-day operations, the sooner you can scale, serve and leverage. We got to a team of around ten staff before we hired our operations manager. There's no doubt in my mind that this was at least five people too late. The growing pains, loss of some key members and overall destructive chaos would have been much less if we'd hired an operations manager earlier.

Start highlighting people now and sell them the vision of running the entire operation one day. Have them shadow you and learn on the job while in their current role. You will get there much sooner and retain existing staff longer this way, as career progression is very important to most team members.

You are always recruiting. We have a rolling recruitment strategy at Progressive, which means we are always hiring. We are always looking for great talent through agencies, and will interview even when roles don't seem vacant but great team members are available. Vacancies and applicants don't align like the sun, moon and stars, and you want great people when they find you. Make a role for them. Ensure you let your team know of this policy so they don't start worrying or gossiping that their role is under threat. Wherever you go, keep your eye out for great talent: coffee shop, shopping centre, leaving other roles, estate agencies, car dealers; always be looking for talent and you will find talent.

• Managing director

A managing director (MD) differs from an operations manager in their ability to be more strategic and visionary. In the UK, the MD and chief executive officer (CEO) are often the same role; in the US the CEO may be a higher level of visionary. We promoted our operations manager to MD as she gained more strategic skills and vision. You can promote internally or you can hire externally. The MD will take a lot of the vision and strategy over from you, freeing your time and mindspace, and de-risking over-reliance on you to drive your enterprise. It will also really help you having another strategist to bounce ideas off and develop a clearer vision and route to get there. The operations manager probably comes before the MD, and they are usually different people because it takes a different skillset to manage than it does to be a visionary.

In today's fast-start business world, there's no reason why you can't have an operations manager or MD in your first five hires. Traditionally, you probably built a bottom-heavy organization of workers and technicians before you hired higher-level management, but I think you will scale and serve better with a more evenly balanced organizational chart, neither top heavy nor bottom heavy.

• Specialists/technicians

The best team will be made up of a visionary, some high-level and highly skilled managers and strategists, and, of course, the very best technicians and specialists. A team of brilliant accountants, lawyers, brokers, marketers, salespeople, advisors and consultants will give you the best results in the shortest time with the minimum wastage. The best will cost a little more, but the results will multiply and the opportunity cost will be significantly less. Settle for nothing and no one but the best and leverage their unique specialist skills.

- **Financiers**

The more access to cash and finance you have, the faster and greater you can scale. For growing your business, buying property and building assets, gaining access to finance is essential. You cannot finance your end-game business on your own. Sure, you can retain a private company, but even that will require reinvestment of profits to grow, which is a form of finance.

Develop and nurture relationships with banks, joint-venture partners, private lenders, crowdfunders, business angels, high-net-worth individuals and bespoke/boutique finance entities. See this as a high-priority KRA and ensure that your access to finance is spread across multiple platforms and opportunities, and that it is liquid and scalable.

3. Service vision (wealth and legacy)

The final section of the MLB is about achieving wealth (legacy) through a service vision. This is the section that shows you how to fund your vision and legacy through passive income generated from assets, and shows you how to diversify your wealth for longevity, protection and compounding. People can argue until the cows come home that money isn't important, and that the best things in life are free, but that is a delusion. In a capitalist society with a fiat system of universal exchange (currency; paper and coins), you either embrace the universal mechanism and have it work for you, or you deny it, work or fight against it and ultimately become a slave to it, or a victim of it.

If you want to grow your wealth so you can live out your vision and create your legacy, you must obey the laws of money and wealth. You will only make money in relation to how you serve and solve for others, so your wealth is measured by your service vision in action. Work out how you can meet your own financial needs and goals through the service of others, and you will have cracked the code of wealth. There are laws that govern money. The wealthy understand and leverage them; the poor are victims of them.

Because money moves from those who value it least to those who value it most, wealth will always move to those who know the laws. The formula for wealth is actually quite simple, and it is shared below. While I have created this formula, it is modelled on the obsessive and enthusiastic study of the wealthiest people on the planet through history, which is a great passion of mine.

Here's the formula:

$$W = (V+E) \times L$$

or:

$$Wealth = (Value + Exchange) \times Leverage$$

Let's look at each element:

- **Value (V)**

Value is the service you give to other people. If you serve and solve, people will receive value/benefit that they will desire more of, pay for, and refer you to others (creating leverage). People are looking for their problems to be solved, and value creation is helping them solve them more quickly and easily. If you're ever struggling yourself financially or emotionally, look more at how you can serve others and solve their problems, and you will have part of the formula for wealth solved.

- ### Exchange (E)

An exchange or transaction has to take place for you to receive money (wealth). You have to give/offer a product, service or idea that someone else perceives highly enough to pay for. But you also have to be able to gratefully receive financial (or other) fair compensation for it. Value without (fair) exchange or transaction will create a financial void in your life, because you will be giving but not allowing receipt, and there will be a lack of fair exchange. Guilt, lack of confidence and imposed religious or social beliefs/ideals make a transaction too one-sided and unsustainable. If you continue to give value without fair exchange or receipt, you will build emotional resentment that will reduce your value creation. You also won't be able to financially sustain the value creation over a long period without receiving fair compensation.

- ### Leverage (L)

Leverage is the scale and speed of serving and solving. The more people you can serve and solve for, the higher the transaction volume and amount will be. The bigger the problem, the higher the transactional amount will be, as fairness of exchange is dictated by the scale and size of the problem. You will only leverage and scale wealth if you have value and fair exchange, because anything that doesn't serve and solve won't scale, or the downsides will scale – reducing reputation and sustainability.

Here's the formula again:

$$W = (V+E) \times L$$

Referrals are a sign of $(V + E) \times L$ working effectively – as is leveraging media such as video, TV and other far-reaching media; leveraging your $(V + E)$. In the world of fibre optics, your $(V + E)$ can leverage very quickly, at the speed of light. You can get 10 million views on YouTube, go viral across multiple social-media platforms and get national or global TV coverage. One-to-many is leverage in great effect.

You could master value and exchange (V + E), but have no scale (L), and you don't have wealth. You could master value and leverage (V + L), but no exchange (E), and you won't allow wealth into your possession. You can master exchange and leverage (E + L), but not value (V), and you won't sustain wealth for long periods; your reputation for not giving value will leverage and wealth will be rebalanced to those giving (V + E) x L.

Honour this formula and the laws of wealth, keep going when you can't immediately see the wealth, stay humble to the process and you will attract and sustain vast wealth.

Here are the forms of wealth that you need to fund your legacy:

- cash flow
- capital
- net worth
- physical assets
- passive income.

• Cash flow

Cash flow is incoming liquid finance. Cash flow pays all fixed costs and overheads on a recurring basis. Whether salary, interest, royalties, commissions or regular drawings/dividends, a steady income stream is vital for sustained wealth. Keep expenses lower than cash flow and you will be able to continue growing towards your vision and legacy. You should look to create multiple streams of cash flow by systemizing one source and building the next. Cash flow comes from assets (property, business, music or intellectual property royalties), from invested time, or non-assets (job, self-managed business, overtime) from spent time.

- **Capital**

Capital is cash or equity 'lumps'. It is less liquid cash, down payment or collateral against an asset. Capital creates protection from variance in asset values and interest rate fluctuations. It is security, debt-cost-reduction and savings, but does not cover monthly residual expenses or disposable costs. At least, it shouldn't. You want to preserve and grow capital at all costs to increase your security and net worth, by saving and investing big lumps of capital as you get them and have cash flow take care of all your ongoing and recurring expenses.

You might have capital in the form of saved cash, equity or deposit in a property, a pension or stocks and shares. If capital is built large enough and preserved well enough, it can produce income. A property can have net rental income, savings can pay interest, a pension may pay a monthly amount and stocks and shares may pay dividends. Use capital to build assets that produce income and you honour and master building wealth. Use capital to buy liabilities or pay monthly expenses and you will soon erode it all. You make capital chunks from drawings and dividends over and above salary, the sale of assets such as property or shares in a business, or by saving disposable income.

- **Net worth**

Net worth is your personal measure of your net asset value. All your assets, minus your total debt and liabilities, leave net worth. This is your financial measure of your progress towards wealth. Because you can't master what you don't measure, start measuring your net worth, as it is your personal wealth KPI. Start where you are at, even if you have a minus net worth, and start investing, building assets and preserving capital.

- **Physical assets**

Physical assets are tangible material items such as gold and precious metals, classic cars, pocket and wristwatches, jewellery, art, wine and antiques. Any material item that goes up in value is a physical asset. Hermès handbags and antique furniture have been known to appreciate in value. You have some of your wealth in physical assets as a protection from extremes such as currency devaluation, acts of war and terror or civil or legal issues. You spread your wealth into physical, material forms to offset other intangible assets, and to de-risk. Use spare cash, leftover capital and disposable income to buy physical assets. You can also merge spending passion with investing profession by investing in the right watches, jewellery and other physical assets that turn spending into investing. I've always had a real passion for watches, and that passion meant I enjoyed researching and learning about the few watches that would preserve capital or even appreciate in value.

- **Passive income**

Passive income is cash flow from assets that you don't have to work for. You don't work hard for your money; your money works hard for you. You systemize the management of your assets with agents, managers and systems, and get a net profit share of the cash flow. Passive income is cash flow that isn't earned but is leveraged. You get passive income from royalties (music, books, IP/licences), businesses that you are not operational in, properties rented out, drawings and dividends not worked for, stocks and shares income, franchise income and so on.

THE MLB THE LIFE LEVERAGE WAY

You now have an entire blueprint, a model and system to follow, to create maximum leverage and mobility to do what you love, when you love, with whom you love. Start now. Follow each part of the blueprint, leveraging as much of the creation of it as you can, and set a plan and timeline as one of your KRAs to have every single aspect of the Mobile Lifestyle Blueprint operational and leveraged.

Live life your way, on your terms, the Life Leverage way. Make the biggest difference you can, serve the most people and leave an amazing legacy thanks to the freedom and global mobility the Mobile Lifestyle Blueprint has given you, as it has given me.

Summary

Follow the Mobile Lifestyle Blueprint step by step to create your ideal mobile lifestyle. Outsource each part of the MLB you can't easily do, and over the next four weeks tick off every single section and subsection to get more done in less time and choose the Life Leverage philosophy as your new way of living, so that you can be, do and have all you want, never wasting a minute of your time and leaving a vast and lasting legacy.

#24 Life Leverage skills (hacks)

There are certain Life Leverage skills that give you maximum compounded benefits. You could call these Life Leverage hacks – extreme productivity for maximum time preservation.

LEARN TO TOUCH-TYPE

According to the *Daily Mail,* the average office worker 'works' on email 2.5 hours a day. That's 81 days a year. According to the *Telegraph,* the average person will type more than 2 million words in their lifetime. The ability to touch-type is a life skill we all need and it can preserve literally years of time with a small, upfront investment of your time. If you went from 30 words a minute to 60 words a minute, you could write 4 million words in your lifetime; that's 2 million extra or 40 published books! You could be earning millions in royalties from the 40 *extra* published books you could write in your lifetime that would take *no extra time* if you learned to touch-type. Or you could halve the amount of words you typed to 1 million, saving 1 million words, which at 30 words per minute is an extra 33,333 minutes saved, or 556 hours, or 23 days.

Learn to touch-type now. Teach yourself on the Internet. Buy a textbook or get a coach; just start now.

LEARN ANOTHER LANGUAGE

Learning another language, or multiple languages, is easier than ever. If English were not your mother tongue, you'd have wanted to learn English because most countries speak English and many of the most powerful, commercial countries speak English as a first language. But, as the world changes, China will become a much more dominant force and, perhaps in the future, learning Chinese in the UK and US will be like the Chinese learning English today.

Get an audio learning programme and have it on in the car (when you're on your own!) and when you are able to NeTime (in a queue, going for a walk, at the gym, etc.). Don't worry about retaining every second of it; just have it on in the background and let it soak into your unconscious mind.

Here's an interesting addition. Heidi, the super-efficient copy-editor and proofreader who's been correcting all my typos and taking out all (well, most) of the expletives, challenged me on learning another language on audio. She said: 'As a language teacher I have to disagree a little with this. It has been proven that you learn languages better from a person face to face, rather than on video or CD. You can back this up with the CD to reinforce it and practise at home and in the car.'

Here's the thing. You can (a) not learn a language at all and keep your brain small, (b) learn a language face to face taking years to get ace, or (c) learn a language in NeTime and preserve all your free time.

You can refine your rough-around-the-edges skills learned on NeTime audio when you travel to the country. The point of NeTime Life Leverage is that you get more done in less time, rather than getting another thing done in time you don't have.

LEARN TO SPEED-READ

It's so simple to double or quadruple your reading speed. Some speed readers can read at 1,500 words per minute, or more. There are many speed-reading courses and books, so start investing in yourself and learn the skills to at least double your reading speed now.

According to a survey done by goodreads.com, the average amount of time that people spend reading is around one hour per day. Taken from the data below, assume that the average person can read 400 words per minute. That's around 24,000 words a day and 8,760,000 words a year. Some sources say that the average is around 300 words a day but I'm giving humanity the benefit of the doubt.

According to forbes.com, the average reading speeds for different types of people are:

- third-grade students = 150 words per minute (wpm)

- eighth-grade students = 250 wpm

- average college student = 450 wpm

- average 'high-level executive' = 575 wpm

- average college professor = 675 wpm

- speed readers = 1,500 wpm

- world speed-reading champion = 4,700 wpm.

Let's add the Life Leverage philosophy to speed reading. If you just doubled your reading speed, which is easily achievable maintaining an 85-per-cent retention rate, then you could read an extra 24,000 words a day. That's an extra 8,760,000 words a year or 350,400,000 in 40 years. This equates to an extra 175 books a year or 7,008 books in the next 40 years. Wow. Get speed-reading, fast.

Here are Rob's fast-start Life Leverage tips to reading at double your speed with just a few minutes' practice a day:

1. Don't say the words in your head.

Do-not-read-the-words-out-loud-in-your-head-like-you're-talking. This takes a little practice but gets your speed right up.

2. Don't read back or reread words or sentences.

This wastes a lot of reading time. Trust your unconscious mind to retain what you weren't conscious of and just keep reading on.

3. Scan the line rather than following it along.

Take in the entire line visually as one piece using your peripheral vision, rather than reading along the line like a teleprompter. You will take in the line much more quickly, and when you aren't reading the words you will consume books like the robot Johnny Five from *Short Circuit*.

I'm no speed-reading expert, but these techniques took just a few minutes and doubled my word speed.

LISTEN TO AUDIO AT DOUBLE SPEED

Possibly one of the biggest benefits and NeTime productivity leverage in my life has been the double compounded benefit of audio, on 2x speed. I've never been a fast reader, and never enjoyed reading that much. At the end of 2005 I started reading non-fiction, personal development books, and it changed my life.

As you get more into learning and reading, the world opens up to you. You read a book and all of a sudden you've bought four more from Amazon and your library gets bigger and bigger with so many books unread and even many books started and on the go at the same time. It can soon become overwhelming. You have to take time out of your day to read, and while it's definitely a high KRA, it's still a sacrifice unless it is what you love to do the most.

When you listen to the same book on audio, you can NeTime. You could be in the gym, travelling, relaxing at home, writing, surfing the Net and social media, even cooking, cleaning or loading the dishwasher, and simultaneously listening to valuable education material that is going straight into your unconscious mind and into your habits. All good. And then I found the 2x button: the little button on iTunes or Audible that doubles the speed of the audio. At first it felt like I couldn't take it in and had the audio on fast-forward. So I started with simple or conceptual books, or books I'd read before, to train my brain to take it in. After a while, 2x speed became the new normal, and normal speed to me now sounds as if the author is having a mild stroke.

You can literally, and in a hands-free, NeTime manner, programme your unconscious mind for success. From January to mid-November of this year this little NeTime technique has enabled me to consume 109 books at an average duration of five hours. That's 545 hours of learning that took no extra time to consume. Start using this technique now. If you are reading this book, you can get it on audio too, from iTunes and Audible.

LISTEN TO AUDIO WITH YOUR CHILDREN

You can use the same NeTime audiobook strategy for and with your children. Get valuable learning audio on in the car as you take them to school. I play golf audio with Bobby in the car, and I think that was part of the reason he was playing golf at the world standard of a seven-year-old when he was only four. What a great gift for your children. Start early and there will be less resistance.

TURN SPENDING INTO INVESTING

If you can turn much of your spending habits into investing habits, you will make 80/20 compounding work for you, save and make possibly hundreds of thousands, or even millions, and have a valuable life skill most don't have.

Think of every material item you buy as a liability/cash-drain, and apply an investor mentality and strategy to each purchase.

Step 1. Can I get by without it?

Step 2. Can I buy second-hand at the bottom of the depreciation curve?

Step 3. Can I turn it into an asset?

Step 4. Can I sell or exchange it before it drops in value further?

Step 5. What's the lowest-cost method of ownership or finance?

You can use the above five steps for almost any material, non-perishable items such as cars, watches, handbags, jewellery, clothing, furniture, AV equipment, even holidays and travel.

Here are the five steps in detail:

Step 1. Can I get by without it?

Do you really need it? Is this a necessary or high-value-to-you purchase, or just a vanity or emotional purchase? Can you drop all spending that gives very short-term or no value, and then focus on spending on the things that give you the highest value? If in doubt, leave it out.

As a reformed spendaholic, something I've learned to do is to make a note of the model number or design of the item I'm about to buy in the moment, with a view to trying to find it online when I get home. Then I'll think 'Do I really need it?' 'Have I ever bought anything like this before and not used it?' 'Will I still want or use this in three years?' 'Is this an 80/20 purchase?'

When I get home I will either find a better deal and save some money (via my researcher), or the emotion of buying the thing I thought I wanted but didn't really need will have gone, and I save myself money by letting it go.

Using these questions will literally save you thousands of pounds a year, which could compound to millions in your lifetime.

Step 2. Can I buy second-hand at the bottom of the depreciation curve?

I really love watches and listening to great-quality music (although my taste in music is questionable). It is of very high value to me to buy a new watch or a new piece of audio equipment, bringing me much sustained joy. But these items are very expensive and, if you're not smart, they can really burn cash.

As I sit here I'm listening to an experimental progressive rock band on my ProAc studio 140mk2s. Beautiful. Such detail, depth and separation. The speakers were around £2,000 new but I bought them for £900 second-hand, and have just sold them on for £700 to make way for my new PMC Fact 8s. These speakers are £6,500 new and I have bought them a year old for £3,500.

Now these speakers might seem like a gratuitous waste of cash, but when you look at the numbers you see a different story. The speakers actually only cost me £200 in the year that I had them, and have given me endless joy and value. The actual cost of a pair of £2,000 speakers to me was 55p a day. I spend £8 a day on coffee. Had I bought these new and owned them for a year, they would have cost me around £800 to £1,000 to own. Speakers actually sound better run in and not new, so it makes sense to let someone else lose £1,000 in a year, and you have cost of ownership of just 55p a day. I've then saved almost half the cost of the new-to-me speakers and will enjoy them at a whole new level. Every six months I can check the residual price, and if they start to drop too much I can sell them and buy another pair that have dropped to a more even depreciation point. The same can be done for second-hand purchases of most goods on eBay or Gumtree.

I could have bought a pair of new speakers for a quarter of the price at £500, had them for one year, and then sold them on for £250. Those speakers would have been of much lower quality and would have actually cost me £50 more to own in the year, so this would have been a false economy. You really can have nicer items and more enjoyable experiences and at the same time preserve more cash or have less eroded through depreciation.

Step 3. Can I turn it into an asset?

It goes to a further level of investment when you can buy something that could go up in value, like watches, jewellery, art or antiques. I've yet to find speakers that go up in value, but as I have a passion for both music and turning spending into investing, I shall continue to watch and learn. The most unique or desired of material items hold value or go up in value, like the Hermès handbag or original designer furniture.

If you buy an all-steel Rolex Daytona, even from new, it will appreciate in value over time – as do some other Rolex models, Patek Philippes and, more recently, some limited-edition novelty Audemars Piguets. You can likely get around £1,000 off for a second-hand Daytona, wear and enjoy a beautiful watch that gives other networking and perception benefits of how others view you, protect your cash from inflation erosion, and make around 7-per-cent gross growth.

I recently purchased a second-hand 1979 Daytona (my birth year) for £25,000 with no paperwork. A Daytona in 1979 would likely have been around £2,000. That is proven residual growth of 12,500 per cent. If it had had the paperwork, it probably would have cost in excess of £30,000. If historical standard Daytonas have grown in value that much, it is likely, though not guaranteed, that yours will too. It is interesting if you compare the purchase of a Daytona to a standard Omega or Breitling – assuming a standard-model Omega or Breitling costs £3,000 and a Daytona £8,000. In three years the Omega or Breitling will be worth around £1,200 to

£1,700, yet the Daytona will be worth £7,000 to £7,500. The Daytona, though requiring more capital, has actually cost £300 to £1,300 less in three years. It compounds further the longer you own it. In ten years the Breitling or Omega is likely to be worth £400 to £800, and the Daytona £9,000 to £10,000 or more. The difference is therefore £3,200 to £4,600 in ownership 'costs'.

Step 4. Can I sell or exchange it before it drops in value further?

Every six to 12 months check the residual values of most of your higher-value material items. Use second-hand sales sites, part-exchange companies and the Internet. Save all the purchase costs of these items in your mSecure private passwords and data folder, and check them. You get double NeTime benefit doing this because (a) you continue to learn about investing and (b) you save or make money timing the purchase and sale of your items.

If I have a watch I thought would hold or appreciate in value start to 'soften' in value, I may sell it on. If I get more for part-exchange I may trade it up, or if there are currency fluctuations I may arbitrage selling in sterling, having bought in dollars, or vice versa. If I feel my spending urge, emotion or addiction overwhelming me, I can research and buy a watch to enjoy wearing and protect the capital or increase its value. That's like being able to eat ice cream and lose weight at the same time!

Step 5. What's the lowest-cost method of ownership or finance?

You hear about people who buy everything on credit and of others who only ever buy anything if they can afford it and have the money. Some people always get loans and some only spend their savings. So which is right? It actually depends.

You should look at total ownership costs, including cost of capital or cost of finance. Whatever you buy, or invest in, has an opportunity cost, where the cash could produce an income elsewhere, or a cost of finance which is the full cost to take out, pay back and pay off the loan. There are often high administration and exit fees on loans that, when you add them to the interest, make the interest rate much higher than it first appeared.

A relevant example now would be a car. Certain car manufacturers offer great lease deals now because of low interest rates and high production volumes. You can quite easily get a £20,000–£30,000 car for not much more than £200 per month plus VAT. Or a £50,000-plus car for £350 to £500 per month plus VAT. There may be a few payments upfront and there is a difference between lease, contract hire, business and personal, so always do your research (or outsource it). There have been some even better deals too, with certain end-of-line models or after bad publicity such as Volkswagen had with the emissions scandal.

Taking the £50,000 car example, depending on the model, if you were to buy new, in two years the car could quite easily be worth £30,000, a depreciation of £20,000. That's £10,000 per year. Plus you'll have a bit of maintenance, costs to sell it, and the cost of the capital held in the depreciating car. In reality, with everything added in, it could have cost you £15,000 a year.

With a similar model on a lease or contract hire, assuming five upfront monthly payments and £500 a month, the two-year cost in total is £14,500. There's no cost of capital, no depreciation cost to you, and no cost of sale (disposal). That's £7,250 a year, less than half the cost of buying the same car new.

If interest rates shot up and the lease became £1,000 a month, then you would think twice, although even at that price it would still be marginally cheaper to lease/contract hire.

If you bought the same £50,000 car three years old for £25,000, it would cost you less to own the car for two years. The depreciation will slow; it may only be another £7,500, which is £3,750 a year. At 5 per cent costs of capital, £25,000 would cost around £2,500 in two years, sale costs might be £2,000, but maintenance will be higher on an older car, say £2,500. In this example the three-year-old car will cost £14,500 over two years, or £7,250 a year. Interestingly, that is the same total, overall cost as leasing the new one.

I could go into much more detail about actual purchasing cost, such as adding costs to insure, loans to purchase second-hand items, storage and security, but the point is clear: always look at the real, sometimes hidden, total cost of ownership and cost of finance of ownership of every item you buy or invest in. If doing this is a passion of yours, you have a great passion–profession, vocation–vacation merge. If it isn't, outsource all the research and quotations.

LEARN TO FLY

There are certain hobby activities that offer huge benefits in all areas of life. This could be getting a racing-car licence, learning magic tricks, performing stand-up comedy or another hobby/skill. I always wanted to fly, having watched every *Airwolf* TV show as a child. It was a dream, and to be honest I never thought it would become a reality. However, thanks to property and the Life Leverage philosophy, I was able to become a qualified helicopter pilot. It has given me endless pleasure and residual benefit: the achievement of a lifelong, childhood (and childish) dream, meeting some amazing people, fantastic high-level networking with wealthy, smart and successful people, self-confidence from having a rare skill, and perhaps a little ego cuddle too.

Flying may or may not give you the same personal and residual benefit it did me. If your desire is to fly, start learning now. If you don't have a lot of disposable cash, learn slowly and steadily and ask that all your gifts from now on be flying lessons. If there is something else you would love to do, that has the Life Leverage philosophy of peripheral, residual benefits, then go and do it. Live your dreams now and justify it with business and network benefits.

Another dream of mine was to be a world-record holder. Sure, there are some quirky world records, so I figured I could find one no one else was really interested in and game the system. That didn't work; there are some hardcore people out there! Then we discovered that the world record for the longest speech was 37 hours. Now I can talk. As my fiancée frequently reminds me, I don't hold the world record for listening. I now hold two world records for the longest speech by one person (52 hours) and the longest team speech marathon (120 hours). I'm sure they'll get beaten, but in the process we raised over £148,000 for our favourite charity, Sue Ryder Care. I got a couple of world records, which makes good dinner conversation and makes me look smarter than I really am. It was great NeTime leverage, and those dozens of hours of content were recorded so that we can repurpose, repackage and leverage into video and audio for years to come. This is passion and profession, vocation and vacation merging for the benefit of many people – and the Life Leverage philosophy in action.

Summary

Life Leverage skills/hacks, such as learning to touch-type and speed-read and listening to audio on double speed will help you to maximize time preservation, so you can work at your ultimate productivity level. Turn spending into investing by buying products that appreciate in value and you'll maximize financial leverage, minimize cash depreciation and still feed your spending addictions and emotions. You really can have fun and grow rich. You may even find time to learn a new skill that you always dreamed of, like flying or scuba diving, while moving towards your vision and merging passion and profession.

#25 Personal Life Leverage

This is the chapter I've been excited to get to and write for you the most, so it is most fitting that it is the last chapter of *Life Leverage*. Thank you for getting this far, it means a lot to me. If I'd have been taught these personal Life Leverage strategies before the age of 25, my life would have had so much more freedom, choice, time and income. Set a goal to outsource as much of your personal life chores as you possibly can, as quickly as you can. Everything that spends or wastes time should be outsourced NOW. It is burning time you can never get back and reducing 80/20 monetary compounding.

Here are the areas of your life you can almost immediately outsource now, to preserve your time and increase your IGV:

- housekeeping/cooking

- gardening

- ironing

- food shopping

- collecting post/prescriptions

- making purchases online including research

- booking travel tickets (flying, trains, etc.)

- driving

- ripping CDs and copying files

- giving instructions, doing complex tasks and research

- undertaking renewals (insurance, change of address, etc.)

- taking the car in for its service/MOT

- looking after the children

- paying bills.

Much of your 'personal' work and chores are holding you back from success, and most people are working too hard to be rich. Any ironing, cleaning, gardening, driving, cooking, housework, car maintenance, shopping and so on bring in zero revenue but take lots of time. Unless you are lucky enough to have a husband or wife who does all that and loves to do all that for you, then you could be spending ten or even 20 hours a week on time wasted (Tw) and time spent (Ts) tasks, trying to save a few pounds but costing yourself thousands.

A millionaire may have an average work time value (IGV) of £5,000 or more per hour. So ten to 20 hours doing these low-level tasks would cost £50,000 to £100,000 of opportunity cost cash. And it would probably cost only £10 to £20 an hour to outsource each of these tasks. People think that millionaires have these luxuries of service because they are millionaires, but the reality is that they became millionaires by valuing their time highly, doing only the highest IGTs and outsourcing/leveraging the rest.

In addition to personal benefit, you get to boost the economy and local employment, you serve more people and therefore you will attract more goodwill and money back to you by outsourcing parts of your life that hold you back and give you a lower IGV.

Start picking them off one by one. Don't see them as a luxury, see them as a necessity. Use family members at first to keep money and time within your family. My mum is our chef and it is great. She is a trained chef, an amazing cook, and my babies get to spend precious time with their grandparents every day. We are going to earn those times back one day in the future. It is a pleasure to pay my mum for that, keep money in the family and preserve precious time. I don't give the ironing to my fiancée, though. Instead, I buy her lots of handbags ...

AND FINALLY...

Thanks to all my mentors who've helped me get out of my own way. Thanks to every author whose books I've read, for sharing and caring enough to want to help others. Thanks to anyone who has the passion and courage to want to teach and help others. It's every ounce of this I could squeeze, plus my own personal crazy-fun life journey, that has helped form the new Life Leverage philosophy. Who knows, perhaps it will become a revolution?

If I can merge my passions and professions, vocations and vacations, then so can you. You might not want to travel the world for half the year and work from one fully synchronized device while your son takes on the golfing world, but whatever it is you love to do, you really can do it from anywhere in the world, whenever you choose. You can spend the summers at home and the nasty winters in the hottest, most beautiful places the world has to offer you, if you choose.

You might not want to break world records, run companies that hire dozens of people that turn over tens of millions of pounds, or own hundreds of houses, but whatever level of wealth and income, scale and autonomy you want, you can have it, if you choose.

You might have children you adore and want to spend all your time with, or you might want to spend more time trying to make more kids or you might want to maximize your independence. You can do which-ever you like, if you choose. You might want to give back or have it all, make money or make a difference, work hard or take it easy, and you can, if you choose.

Follow the concepts, strategies, tactics, systems and blueprint in *Life Leverage*, and you can be it all, do it all, have it all, and be an inspiration and service to a vast number of people.

Good luck with it all, and keep me posted on how you get on.

Summary

Your 'personal' work and chores are holding you back from success. Fact. Get someone else to do tasks such as ironing, food shopping, cleaning, gardening and driving, so you can focus on more important IGTs. Trying to save money on the little jobs is actually costing you thousands, when you think of your IGV. Start outsourcing now. Your choice.

Afterword: What are you going to do now?

To know and not to do ...

... is not to know.

So now you have a good level of knowledge to get out there and live the Life Leverage philosophy for business and pleasure, merging vocation and vacation, passion and profession and getting more done in less time, outsourcing everything and creating your ideal mobile lifestyle. But of course you know that this is not the end of the road, this is just the beginning. The rest is up to you, so go out there and make a difference.

I hope that we will talk in the future and you will be telling me your stories of action, leverage and success. When all is said and done, more is said than done, and I have faith that you are one of the doers and not the talkers.

> 'It's easy to do, but also easy not to do.'

I hope you choose the easy part.

Get perfect later. Fail forward fast. Think big, start small. Start now.

I feel grateful and privileged to be part of your journey and would welcome us staying in contact. Please follow me here, send me a message, write a review on Amazon, pose me a question or have a good rant:

www.facebook.com/robmooreprogressive

You can also add me on Twitter:

www.twitter.com/robprogressive

If you think this book could help people you care about, please recommend it to them. Someone cared about me enough in 2015 and recommended a book to me that changed my life completely. I wasn't really a reader back in 2015, and Mike Wildman, who owned a gallery that hung some of my art, persisted in getting me to read *Think and Grow Rich* by Napoleon Hill.

Wow. That book shook me but inspired me. Thank you, Mike. I will always remember that moment. Please share that gift with others so together we can make a difference.

I promised you two gifts at the start of this book. One of them is shared twice in the book, just in case you came right to the end to find it before reading the entire book. The other is a free subscription to 'The Disruptive Entrepreneur' podcast. This is a podcast that extends the Life Leverage philosophy further and give tools, techniques and hacks on productivity, leverage, scaling of your enterprise, merging passion and profession and personal and financial growth. It's not for the faint-hearted.

http://www.robmoore.com/podcast/

Just one final thing ...

Mark Homer isn't the real name of my friend who 'leveraged' me for my GCSE results. No harm was done to Mark Homer or any other Mark Homers in the writing of this book.